Sheffield
In Verse

collected and edited by
Peter Machan

"City of Bards" should be our borough's name,
Since Montgomery gained for it lasting fame;
How near is Sheffield to Apollo's throne!
The sacred nine, forsooth, delight in smut,
So much they honour this our *town of soot*.

The Young Byronian, 1856

Thanks to: Joan Jones, Nuala Keller, Don Alexander and the ever helpful and patient staff of the Local Studies Library, Sheffield.

The rights of the original copyholder are upheld and where attempts to discover the location of this person has been unsuccessful they should contact the publisher.

© Peter Machan 2004

Printed and published by:
ALD Design & Print
279 Sharrow Vale Road
Sheffield S11 8ZF

Telephone 0114 267 9402
E:mail a.lofthouse@btinternet.com

ISBN-13: 978-1492950738

ISBN-10: 1492950734

First Published October 2004

All rights reserved
No part of this publication may be reproduced, stored in a retrieval system or transmitted in any form or by any means, electronic, mechanical, photocopying, recording or otherwise, without prior written permission of the publisher.

Contents

Introduction; 'City of Bards' 1

The Changing face of Hallamshire

Sheffield, Andrew Gregory, 1989 8
Sheffield, John Holland, 1851..9
The Lord's Oak, W.H. Sterndale..10
Sheffield, Anna Seward..12
The Old Grammar School, Rev. Inchbald..13
Shirecliffe, Ebenezer Elliiott..14
Walkley, Ebenezer Elliott 15
Wincobank Hill, J. Nixon...16
Hunters Bar, anon..17
The Rivers of Hallamshire, Ebenezer Elliott...18
The Sheaf & Sheffield Park. John Holland 19
Mary Queen Scots..21
Ribbledin, Ebenezer Elliott 22
My Native Rivelin, Henry Waterfall...23
The Old Home by the Don, E Darbyshire 25
City of Steel, Author Unknown, 1980 26
The Contrast, James Wills, 1827 28
Urban Inflation, Andrew Gregory, 1989 32
The Beauty of Sheffield Plate, L.du Garde Peach. 1947..............................33
Edwardian Sunday, Broomhill, John Betjeman,1960.................................35
Regeneration, Hazel Clarke, 1995 37
Sheffield, Andrew Gregory, 1989 39
Sheffield, Farewell! E. Darbyshire,1885 40

Moments in Time

Castle Inscription 42
Sheffield Castle, Francis Buchanan, 1882 43
Sheffield Manor, Francis Buchanan, 1882 45
Steam Power, Ebenezer Elliott...47

iii

Norfolk Street Riots, Joseph Mather, 1795 48
The Invitation, Joseph Senior, 1882 50
Opening of Firth Park, E. Darbyshire, 1875 51
Welcome to the Prince and Princess of Wales, John Hall, 1875 53
A Street Scene, William Dowsing, 1910 55
Opening of the New Town Hall, Author Unknown, 1897 56
The Old Queen's Visit, G.C. Moore, 1897 57
Sir Henry Coward, Ellen Styring, ... 59
Street March of the Sheffield Boy's Brigade, E. Downing, 1906 60
Cry From The City, C.A. Renshaw, 1916 62
Coles Corner, Ebenezer Downing, 1906 64
Beatlemania, S. Alexander, 1966 66
Coal, Hazel Clarke 1990 67
Pickets at Orgreave, 'J' 1985 68
Song of the Picket Lines, Miner's Wife, 1984 69
Death of the Rag and Tag, Ralph Thickett, 1973 70

Grime and Poverty

Sheffield, William Carpenter, 1877 72
The Old Canal, Wiliam Dowsing, 1910 75
Dirty Sheffield, anon 76
Hungry Forties, T'owd Hammer, 1937 77
The Tip, William Dowsing, 1910 78
File Hewer's Lament, Joseph Mather, 1780 79
Nickerpecker's Complaint 80
Song of the Men on the Parish at Hollow Meadows 81
Sheffield Street Song 81

A Working Life

T'Sheffield Cutler, L. du Garde Peach, 1948 84
The Reeve's Tale, Chaucer 85
The Merry Travellers, anon 87

Buffer Girl, Margaret Morley, 1996 88
The Song of the City of Steel, L. du Garde Peach, 1948 89
Loisin' Day, anon 90
Shepherd Wheel, P. Fairclough, 1992 92
The Cutler's Daughter, E. Darbyshire, 1885 93
The Grinder, Ebenezer Elliott, 1815 95
Tally i o The Grinder, Trad. 19th Century 96
Grinder's Hardships, Trad. 19th Century 97
File Cutter's Lament, anon 99
The Steam Hammer, John Hall, 1862 101
John Brown & Co., R.N. Ryan, 1861 103
The Whittlesmith's Lamentation, Joseph Senior, 1882 106
Norton Scythesmith's Song, Trad, 1814 107
Cutler's Poetry, 17th Century 108
The Toll Keeper, John Hall, 1864 109

Death and Disaster

The Cholera Monument, James Montgomery, 1832 112
A Hopeless Case, P. Scott, 1864 115
Inscriptions on Tombstones of Flood Victims, 1864 117
Lines on the Great Flood, J.B. Geoghegan, 1864 119
Sheffield Blitz, A.F.S., 1941 122
To The People of Sheffield, S. May, 1940 126
Remembering Mi Amigo, Anderson Family, 2002 127
Memorial to William Hobson, 1815 129
Gravestone to a Favourite Horse 130
Local Epitaphs 131
Sheffield Cemetery, L. Smith, 1854 132

Fun and Frolics, Love and Life

The Rose & Crown, anon 136

Little Sheffield Feast, anon 137
Yorkshire Ways, C.A. Renshaw, 1922 138
The Sheffield Cutler's Song, Trad. 18th Century 140
The Jolly Grinder, Trad. 19th century 142
Botanic Gardens, E.Eaton, 1867 144
Sheffield Park, Trad. 18th Century 146
The Sheffield Apprentice, Trad. 18th Century 148
Handsworth Sword Dancers, J.Siddall, 1920 150
Wednesdayites, Hazel Clarke, 1995 151
Lyall & Needham, Footballers, 1904 152
The Whit Walk, Grace Leeder-Jackson 154

The Heroic and the Villainous

The Rhyming Couplets of Worksop, Pigot, 15th Cent. 156
Talbot at the Siege of Orleans, Shakespeare 159
The Death of John Talbot, William Shakespeare 160
Epitaph to 6th Earl of Shrewsbury 161
The Battle of Brunanburgh, 10th Century 163
The Dragon of Wantley, Trad, 17th Century 164
The New Dragon of Wharncliffe, S. Roberts, 1838 170
Bill Brown, the Poacher, Trad. 19th Century 172
Charlie Peace Rhyme 174
Frank Fearne, Joseph Mather, 1782 175
Steven's and Lastley's Execution, Joseph Mather, 1790 176
Sir Francis Chantrey, Ellen Styring 179
The Ballad of Spence Broughton the Highwayman, Trad 181

References to Collected Works and Sources

Index of First Lines 184

FOREWORD
by Ian McMillan

Welcome to this collection of poems about Sheffield, written over hundreds of years and in lots of different styles. Some of these poems rhyme, some don't; some you can dance to, some you could sing; you'll laugh at some and you'll cry at others, and that's how a book of poems should be.

A collection like this is a great map of a city, much better than your average street plan, because poems contain hopes and fears and memories and stories and they bring a place to life. In this book we can trace the history of Sheffield and the history about how Sheffield thinks about itself, and that's really why books like this are important: they reflect a place back on itself like local papers and local radio do, they fill us in on a kind of history that tends to be ignored by the history books, and they make beautiful poetry out of ordinary extraordinary lives.

So enjoy this book; it's a great book about a great city, and that's high praise indeed coming from a Barnsley fan!

Ian McMillan

www.ian-mcmillan.co.uk

Introduction
'City of Bards'

Although other authors have made collections of the works of Sheffield poets, this, as far as I know, is the first time that an anthology of the many poems and verses relating to Sheffield itself has been put together, and many of those included here have never been reprinted since their original publication, often in the nineteenth century. They deserve to be better known and enjoyed.

There are some gems here, but I make no claims regarding the general quality of the verses in this collection. There again, neither did most of their local writers. Henry Waterfall starts the preface to his delightfully produced collection of poems entitled 'Rivelin Rhymes' in 1880 with the following disclaimer-

> *'It would have been better if my verses had been smoother, not so fragmentary and more in accordance with the requirements of acknowledged poetry; but I have not made much progress in the art, so I must let them go as they are.'*

This is the great joy of collecting together examples of poetry and verse which share a location as their theme. Most of the writers, I do not call them poets, were locals who had little formal education but felt they had something to say, and, tortuous and ham-fisted as many of their efforts were, they are invariably fascinating and enjoyable. Most of the verses were written, not with an eye to posterity, but as an emotional response to a particular event. In some cases, in days long before photography and sound recording, these poems give us some of the clearest insights into the ordinary people's feelings and attitudes towards where they lived and the events they witnessed. Like those who today suffer the sad loss of a dear relative these writers turned to verse rather than prose as the medium which could best express their feelings.

The themes are familiar and are reiterated over again. Most of the writers tend to be backward-looking, bemoaning the changes that have taken place since their childhoods or their grandparents' days. Their views were not necessarily complimentary to authority and frequently they were at odds with the establishment. For several writers working in the turbulent early years of the nineteenth century the verses formed a powerful weapon of political propaganda, although of these only Ebenezer Elliott, campaigning in his writings and speeches against the iniquities of the Corn Laws which kept the price of bread at an inflated price, was a nationally known figure. More entertaining, perhaps, were the scurrilous verses of Joseph Mather, the Sheffield Broadsheet Balladeer, who spent several spells in the local gaol in Scotland Street when his doggerel verses were deemed libellous by their affronted targets.

Mather had unimpeachable Sheffield credentials. Born in 1737 in a miserable hovel in Cack Alley, a jennel which ran from Lambert Street to Westbar, he was apprenticed as a filecutter. His stocky, well-built figure became familiar throughout the streets and inns of the town, singing his ballads and distributing broadsides. Something of a showman, it is said that he was a habitué of the racecourse at Crookes where he would appear performing from the back of a cow. His doggerel verses lampooning the characters of the day or vilifying the pompous are not without merit and are invaluable in giving us an insight into issues of the day which concerned the working man. He died in 1804 and his 'works' were collected and printed in 1811. Outstanding amongst those verses produced by contemporaries of Mather, whose names are generally unknown, are the collection of 'folk' lyrics relating to the generally arduous working conditions of the Sheffield tradesmen, and of the Sheffield grinders in particular. Songs like *'To Be a Sheffield Grinder'* and *'Tally-I-O The Grinder'* graphically portray the perception of the working man's lot in these early days of the industrial revolution. Many of these songs were rejuvenated in the 1960s when they were written into the script of Allan Cullen's *'Stirrings in Sheffield on Saturday Night'*.

At entirely the opposite end of the social scale three writers who can truly be termed poets, earned for Sheffield a reputation as something of a literary centre in the first half of the nineteenth century.

John Holland

Although they are generally disregarded and little read today, their local standing at the time can be appreciated by the fact that two of them are the only Sheffield worthies to ever be commemorated by full length statues. These were John Holland, Ebenezer Elliott and James Montgomery.

Of the three only John Holland can claim true belonging to Sheffield, being born in 1794 in a house on the hillside in the Park not far from the Manor Lodge; a house in which he lived for much of his life and which, amazingly, still stands. A stalwart of the church and of the closely-knit intellectual circle of the time, Holland's interests were broad, perhaps too broad to enable him to focus on creating the quality of writing which would have brought lasting distinction. As well as poetry Holland wrote eleven volumes of biography, numerous articles of local antiquarian interest and a number of scientific works, such as '*A Memoir of the History and Cultivation of the Gooseberry*' and '*The History and Description of Fossil Fuel*'. In fact there seem to have been few subjects to which he was not prepared to turn his attention for in 1870 he produced his '*Handy Book on Matters Matrimonial*' ; a curious subject from a lifelong batchelor. He died at the Mount, Broomhill, in 1872.

It is as a hymn writer rather than as a poet that James Montgomery won national acclaim, and many of his compositions, such as '*Angels from the Realms of Glory*' are familiar today. There were, however many facets to his long career. Born in 1771 in Ayreshire, Scotland, he came to Sheffield only following a chance reading of an advertisement for a journalist on the radical Sheffield paper, '*The Register*'. Following the enforced expatriation of the editor, Joseph Gales, Montgomery took over editorial

James Montgomery

control, changing the name to *'The Iris'*. He maintained, however, the radical stance of the paper and consequently found himself frequently at odds with the establishment and spent several uncomfortable spells in York prison. Montgomery was uncritically appreciated as the leader of the somewhat narrow intellectual circle in the town and his unstinting campaigning on behalf of many humanitarian causes fully justifies his fine monument now being given a prominent position beside the Cathedral. His poetry unfortunately only rarely features topics of local interests, for amongst his best favoured works are *'Greenland'*, *'The World Before the Flood'* and *'The Pelican Island'*, all of which sold prolifically and yielded a handsome income. Montgomery died, aged 83, in 1854.

Ebenezer Elliott

As a poet, when he was writing for the love of it rather than as a political agitator, Ebenezer Elliott was by far the finest writer of the three. Although Elliott's early life was spent in working at the steel works founded by his father in Rotherham he always displayed a sensitivity to nature and to the natural beauty of his surroundings and these are the first impulses towards his early poetry. He only came to Sheffield, with his wife and nine children, at the age of forty on the complete failure of his steel business and consequent bankruptcy. He started out again and this time made a success of the business and embraced a love for Sheffield's hidden beauties. Becoming convinced that the root of many of the country's social ills were the Corn Laws which kept the price of bread at an artificially high price to protect the farmers, Elliott turned his talent to producing vitriolic verses in condemnation of this evil, becoming known for ever afterwards as 'The Corn Law Rhymer'. Fortunately Elliott also wrote voluminously about his adopted town.

As Mary Walton states;-

He deserves to be remembered by Sheffield people because he tried to put into words the peculiar emotional response of which most lovers of Sheffield are aware; a response to its odd mixture of natural grandeur and man-made squalor, of clanging forges and Cyclopean furnaces and picturesque street names and general drabness relieved by accidentally attractive groupings of streets and buildings.*

This is exactly what the best of the poems in this collection do.

If Mather had led the way for ordinary townsfolk to express themselves in verse there were many keen to follow his example. So prolific was the outpouring of verse by untutored bards by the mid nineteenth century that an anonymous writer who published a pamphlet in the name of 'The Young Byronian' in 1856 satirised them in scathing terms as follows:-

But where's the town that can with ours compete?
Rhymesters reside in almost every street.
The Muse's courtiers never are to seek-
New ones are manufactured every week.
When a bard is with new honours crown'd
Numbers of would-be poets flock around
To learn the path in which the fav'rite trode,
And try their chances in the self same road;
And toil and sweat to make some couplets ring,
For greater blockheads than themselves to sing.

---

* 'Sheffield, Its Story and its Achievements' Mary Walton, 1948.

Most of the results of these labours are now lost and we only have a few verses which were published as broadsides or pamphlets in the early nineteenth century. In the latter half of the century, however, it became fashionable for writers to have their collections published as bound collections. Today we would refer to these as 'vanity' publications, although the subscription lists printed in some of these anthologies suggests that they had a wide local support. The list of over two hundred subscribers in the front of Joseph Senior's 1882 *'Smithy Rhymes and Stithy Chimes',* for example opens with Lord Wharncliffe and includes virtually every industrialist of note in the town. Whilst many of these anthologies form an extremely attractive addition to the bookshelf they contain some pretty indifferent writing. The authors did not restrict themselves as far as subject matter was concerned but wrote about anything that took their fancy and much of it is, not surprisingly given the Victorian date, extremely sentimental. E. Darbyshire, who had the opticians on Bow Street, includes poems in his *'Ballads Poems and Recitations'* of 1885 entitled *'My Hobby Horse', 'How Can She Care for Me'* and the extraordinary *'I'm Standing at Your Grave, Mary'* . Many of these writers attempt to reproduce the 'Old Shevvild' dialect. I have avoided reproducing all but a few of the earliest authentic dialect pieces as they are generally extremely laboured and laborious to read.

I just hope that you have as much enjoyment from reading this anthology as I have had in collecting it!

The Changing Face of Hallamshire

Sheffield

by Andrew Gregory, 1989*

Sheffield was the place
The place where it happened
Half the steel in the world
The most productive square mile
The whole globe cut its meat
With what this place gave

Rock-hard hero
Of that tallest of tales

You were History

The Prince of Wales watching the casting of an Ingot of Crucible Steel at Thomas Firth's Norfolk Works in 1875

---

* From 'Regeneration', a collection of poems to accompany the exhibition of the same name at the Untitled Gallery, October 1989.

Sheffield from 'The Diurnal Sonnets' by John Holland, 1851

In this very nicely constructed sonnet do we get the impression that Holland, one of Sheffield's most celebrated romantic poets, is apologising for rather than eulogising his native town? Although there is a professed feeling of belonging, he clearly feels himself well removed from the honest sons of toil who brought it *'just renown'*. Is Holland here being somewhat patronising towards the *'good, old-fashioned town'*; and what are the town's unsurpassed *'social virtues'*? We are left to wonder.

East Prospect of Sheffield by Samuel and Nathaniel Buck, 1745

Hail Sheffield! Happy, good, old-fashion'd town,
   Among thy living thousands, as a son,
   I pay the filial praise, for thou hast won,
   'Midst cities of best fame, a just renown:
What, if less glittering be thy merchant crown-
   Thy social virtues are surpass'd by none:
What, if ships crowd not the swol'n Sheaf or Don,
   Their ancient worth still mingles with thine own:
   O'er beds of coal and iron still they flow;
   Their sluices turn the grinder's rapid wheel;
   They give keen temper to the cutting steel;
   Hail then, the hardy, honest, manly worth,
   To which the homes of Industry give birth,
Where anvils ever ring, and forge-fires ever glow!

The Lord's Oak
by William Handley Sterndale, Early 19th Century.*

It was during the mid seventeenth century, when the local ironmasters needed all the wood that they could get from the local woodlands to convert to charcoal and the Howards, the Dukes of Norfolk, were intent on exploiting the maximum revenue from their local holdings, that the ancient and venerable trees of Rivelin Chase and Sheffield Park were felled. The Rivelin oaks were sold to Lionell Copley who ran forges at Rockley and Attercliffe. This caused considerable ill-feeling and a local rhyme sums up, in terser terms, the sentiment of the poem which follows;

> If Mr. Copley had never been born,
> Or in his cradle had died,
> Loxley Chase had never been torn
> And many a brave wood beside.

It is said, however, that the Lord's Oak itself, a massive tree with a bole of twelve yards in girth, survived until 1690. Its exact location, though somewhere at the top of the valley, is unrecorded. The poet, incidentally, must surely have looked with despair on the industrial developments that were to pollute 'the Don's translucent floods' within a few years!

The 10 foot **'Iron Man'** in Bowden Housteads woods symbolises the link between the woodlands and the iron industry

* Quoted in Hunter's 'Hallamshire' Gatty Edition, 1869

In all their pride still wave the Wharncliffe's woods,
   Still o'er their bowers the summer dews descend,
In freshness flow the Don's translucent floods,
   High o'er whose banks the rifted rocks ascend;
   Still all his hidden brooklets rippling wend
Through mossy banks, and murmur as they flow
   Where pensile flowers like bashful virgins bend
To see their beauties in the waves below,
That kiss their perfumed lips, and in their blushes glow.

But in the Riveling's solitary vale,
   Where all seems dead and silent save the stream,
Where no tree waves its branches in the gale,
   Nor scarce a blossom woos the summer beam;
   The pilgrim pauses, as the wandering dream
Of time-sepulchred years o'er memory's plain
   Slowly returns......pursuing still the theme,
He marks the spot where once in grandeur stood
The lordly Oak, sole monarch of the solitude.

Amidst the silence and the loneliness
   Of that dark valley where no leaf appears,
He stood, the sovereign of the wilderness,
   And flourish'd greenly, and without compeers,
   In strength and beauty, and adorn'd by years;
The earth his footstool Heaven his canopy
   No Druid's rites he saw, no victim's tears;
But widely there his giant arm unfurl'd
His green and bloodless banner o'er a peaceful world.

Sheffield by Anna Seward[*]

What a pompous and thoroughly charmless outpouring this is, not untypical of the work of Anna Seward, the so-called 'Swan of Lichfield' who was born in the village of Eyam. It is not surprising that even Walter Scott, on being bequeathed most of her poetry, pronounced it 'execrable'. Compare it with John Holland's pieces on the same theme.

> Sheffield, smoke involved; dim where she stands
> Cirled by lofty mountains, which condense
> Her dark and spiral wreaths to drizzling rains
> Frequent and sullied; as the neighbouring hills
> Ope their deep veins, and feed their cavern'd flames.
> No aerial on Sheffield's arid moor
> Ere wove the floral crowns, or smiling stretch'd
> The shelly sceptre;- there no poet roved
> To catch bright inspirations. Blush, ah blush,
> Thou venal genius of these outraged groves,
> And thy apostate head with thy soil'd wings
> Veil! Who hast thus thy beauteous charge resign'd
> To habitants ill-suited; hast allow'd
> Their rattling forges, and their hammers' din,
> And hoarse rude throats to fright the gentle train
> Dryads and fair-haired Naiades;- the song
> Once loud as sweet of the wild woodland choir
> To silence;- disenchant the poet's spell,
> And to a gloomy Erebus transform
> The destined rival of Tempean vales.

[*] Quoted in Hunter's 'Hallamshire', Gatty Edition, 1864.

The Old Grammar School from 'The Borough'
by Rev. Dr. Inchbald late 18th Century*

Where sooty tops of clanking tilts arise,
Which heave their smoky volumes to the skies;
Where the red furnace boils with hollow roar
And melts to fiery wave the massy ore;
Where cheerful labour whistles o'er the wheel,
Which smooths to keenest edge the stubborn steel;
T'was in that mart of ancient honest fame
(How ancient, Fox, let Chaucer's verse proclaim,)
T'was there to form aright our tender youth,
Instruction mild poured forth the light of truth,
And wayward nature first was taught to bear
The yoke of thraldom in a master's care.

Pleased, I remember, and forever must,
Till memory's powers lie slumbering in the dust,
The wall-encircled court that day withstood,
Low sunk, in which our noisy prison stood;
The low-arched porch of ancient gothic date,
The modest portal of our prison gate;
(In piteous case, disastrous to disclose,
There oft I've seen the little lingerers pause,
With artful head the truant tale contrive,
To Chadwick's frown all tremblingly alive);
The gloomy entrance, with its double door,
The scooped threshold, and the deep-worn floor,
The low-ranged forms to glossy smoothness wore,
With many a name all hacked and mangled o'er,
The high raised wall that half shut out the day,
And fixed attention, while it bounded play.

This is a print of the boy's Charity School in East Parade. Built in 1825, it still stands. The School referred to in the poem, however was the even older Grammar School, which stood near Townhead Street.

* Quoted in Hunter's 'Hallamshire', 1819, and repeated, in a Bowdlerised form, in John Derry's 'Story of Sheffield', 1914.

Shirecliffe from 'The Ranter'   by Ebenezer Elliot*

This poem by the old Corn Law Rhymer really appeals to me, especially as I must be one of the sluggards whom Elliott is admonishing, since I'm rarely up with the lark! The view he is describing is from, surprisingly, Shirecliffe, which was then noted as a beauty spot. The 'Ranter', which is the real subject of the piece, was a preacher who had come here to preach under the 'Gospel Tree', an old ash which stood at the top of the hill. The gospel he preached consisted of a denunciation of the Corn Laws and their supporters.

Shirecliffe, from a Sketch by C. Thompson, From Pawson and Brailsford's Guide, 1862.

Up! sluggards up! the mountains one by one
Ascend into light, and slow the mists retire
From vale and plain. The cloud on Stannington
Beholds a rocket-No, 'tis Morthen spire.
The sun is risen! cries Stanedge, tipped with fire.
On Norwood's flowers the dewdrops shine and shake.
Up! sluggards up! And drink the morning breeze;
The birds on cloud-left Osgathorpe awake,
And Wincobank is waving all his trees
O'er subject towns, and farms and villages
And gleaming streams and woods, and waterfalls.
Up! climb the oak-crowned summit! Hoober Stand
And Keppel's Pillar gaze on Wentworth's halls
And misty lakes that brighten and expand,
And distant hills that watch the western strand.

* Quoted in Pawson & Brailsford's 'Illustrated Guide to Sheffield', 1862.

Up! trace God's footprints where they paint the mould
With heavenly green, and hues that blush and glow
Like angel's wings, with skies of blue and gold
Stoop to Miles Gordon on the mountain's brow.
Behold the great Unpaid! the prophet. Lo!
Sublime he stands beneath the gospel tree,
And Edmund stands on Shirecliffe at his side!
Behind him sinks, and swells, and spreads a sea
Of hills and vales and groves. Before him glide
Don, Rivelin, Loxley, wandering in their pride
From heights that mix their azure with the cloud.

Walkley from 'Rural Rhymes'
by Ebenezer Elliott

Sheffield is a wonderful place to watch the weather as it sweeps in from the west and this piece gives a masterful impression of the gathering evening storm. Who Sarah and William Adams might be I have no idea!

Sarah and William Adams! Here we stood
Roof'd by the cloud which cast his frown between
Wardsend and Loxley's moorlands. From the wood
Of one-starr'd Grenno, like a sea unseen,
The wind swept o'er us, seeming in his might,
To shake the steadfast rocks; while, rushing keen
Beyond the edge of darkness, stormy light,
As from a leaguewide trumpet, on the scene
A cataract of glory pour'd; and, bright
In gloom, the hill-tops islanded the night
Of billowy shade around us. Vale and hill,
Forest and cloud, were restless as a fight;
They seemed as they would never more be still;
While, anchor'd over all, the high poised kite
Saw the foame'd rivers dash their blue and white.

Wincobank Hill by John Nixon, 19th Century.

If any poem in this collection conjures the vision of the vast changes which industrialisation brought to the landscape in the late nineteenth century it is this one. It is difficult to reconcile this view of Wincobank Hill as a serene haven with the despoiled heap which now stands marooned amongst housing developments, overlooking the industrial sprawl of the Don Valley and Meadowhall!

When summer comes on and the sweet month of June,
With its lovely attractions puts all things in tune,
If the artist should try he would fail in his skill,
To pencil the beauties of Wincobank Hill.

On natures vast grandeurs we look with delight,
The scene all around is a beautiful sight,
The flowers with fragrance the air they do fill,
These are the productions of Wincobank Hill.

How lovely, delightful, transporting it looks,
All around we see forests, meadows and brooks,
Where sweet purling waters down the valley do rill,
These are the beauties of Wincobank Hill.

No noise nor confusion through the district is heard
But the sweet noise of the warbling bird.
The schoolboys with echoes the air they do fill,
That is all that molests us on Wincobank Hill.

Then who would not wish on this hill to reside,
Where nature shines forth in the noblest of pride.
Our hearts unto Him should with gratitude fill,
Who gives us these blessings on Wincobank Hill.

Hunters Bar.   Author unknown.

I collected most of the poems for this anthology from old books that I bought from second hand bookshops or perused in the Local Studies Library. I found this one pasted on the wall of Two Steps chip shop on Sharrow Vale Road! The lovely photograph of Hunters Bar in the early 20th Century was in the furniture shop.

The voice of nature here prevailed
Before the day of tram or car,
When children few went off to school
    At pleasant Hunters Bar.

A school now stands where bluebells grew,
A hundred noises throb and jar,
In Sheffield's suburb by the Cliffe,
    The modern Hunters Bar.

And children in their hundreds learn,
And sing and play and shout 'hurrah1'
While Porter flows as e'er it flowed,
    Through dear old Hunters Bar.

Along Sheffield's suburban fringe,
Where wood and park and school there are,
Where Pennine's foothills lose their height,
    Stands ancient Hunters Bar.

'Twas a hamlet picturesque,
With Endcliffe's tow'ring ridge not far,
Weary travellers from the hills
    Took rest at Hunters Bar.

Few ancient landmarks still survive,
For time and man both make and mar,
But Porter's babbling, swirling stream
    Still flows through Hunters Bar.

The Rivers of Hallamshire, from 'The Village Patriach' by Ebenezer Elliott

The Rivers of Hallamshire

Five rivers, like the fingers of a hand,
Flung from black mountains, mingle, and are one,
Where sweetest valleys quit the wild and grand,
And eldest forests, o'er the silven Don,
Bid their immortal brother journey on,
A stately pilgrim watched by all the hills.
Say, shall we wander, where, through warriors' graves,
The infant Yewden, mountain-cradled, trills
Her Doric notes? Or, where the Locksley raves
Of broil and battle, and the rocks and caves
Dream yet of ancient days? Or, where the sky
Darkens o'er Rivilin, the clear and cold,
That throws his blue length, like a snake, from high?
Or, where deep azure brightens into gold
O'er Sheaf, that mourns in Eden? Or, where roll'd
On tawny sands, through regions passion-wild,
And groves of love, in jealous beauty dark,
Complains the Porter, Nature's thwarted child,
Born in the waste, like headlong Wiming? Hark!
The poised hawk calls thee, Village Patriach!
He calls thee to his mountains! Up, away!
Up, up, to Stanedge! Higher still ascend,
Till kindred rivers, from the summit grey,
To distant seas their course in beauty bend,
And, like the lives of human millions, blend
Disparted waves in one immensity!

The Manor Tower and The Sheaf from 'Sheffield Park'
by John Holland

These fragments of a long piece written by John Holland in the early years of the nineteenth century, at a time when the pace of change was growing to a crescendo, hark back to a more idyllic, earlier age of his boyhood. It was a scene he would have known well for he was born in a cottage in the Park in 1794. It's a delightful piece, full of imagery, and, as a school boy who well remembers hunting for minnows in the Sheaf, it has personal resonance. With the waters of the Sheaf being harnessed to drive dozens of water wheels it was not surprising that it became little more than a feeble trickle in the height of summer.

Ruins of the Manor Lodge, 1795

The Manor Tower

XIII

There was - remembrance dimly paints its form, -
A lofty turret nodding to the storm;
Wrapped in a vest of ivy, proud it stood,
As some grey wreck that has survived the flood;
There angry winds in furious skirmish met,
Swept its green cloak and mouldering parapet -
Seem'd as with fingers rude to mock at crime,
And pluck'd the wizard beard of hoary time:
The bat here claimed hereditary right;
The owl its tenant screamed, unscarred at night:
At last, like age weigh'd down with years, it fell,
Nor left a vestige of its fate to tell.

The Sheaf

XXVIII

No trees umbrageous stretch their sylvan ranks
Along my native Sheaf's adjacent banks,
Nor always full and flowing does the stream
Reflect the clouds and skies and solar beam;
Rapid, and swollen, and turbid, oft it rolls,
When winter's stormy squadrons, from the poles,
Hither their snows and treasured waters bring,
Deluge the hills and gush from every spring;
But when the fiery dog-star fervid reigns,
Shrunk and exhaled the feeble streamlet drains;
And schoolboys, dry-shod, when their tasks are sped,
For worthless minnows search its pebbly bed.

XXIX

Ascending now, the river's course to mark,
Along the western limit of the Park,
We pass a hill with scarce a verdant trace,
Where flaming ovens burnt along its base
Globes hot as Etna, whence the glowing coke
Belch'd, from each fiery crater, clouds of smoke,
Which formed, beneath the sapphire arch of night,
A dusky canopy of lurid light;
Now cold, disrupted, spread their fireless wombs,
Like the rent fragments of exploded bombs,
Such as are oft from hostile mortars thrown
Within the walls of some bealeagured town.

Inscription in the Grounds of Queen's Tower 1830s*

When Samuel Roberts had built Queen's Tower below Norfolk Park in the 1830s he instructed the landscape architect Robert Marnock to lay out the grounds. A feature in this design was a ruin rebuilt from the remains of the Manor, including a portion of wall and window. This verse was carved on a marble tablet nearby.

The Mary Queen of Scots window in the Cathedral Chapter House.

Alone, here oft may Scotia's beauteous Queen
Through tears, have gazed upon the lovely scene;
Victim of villainy, of woman's hate,
Of fiery zeal, of wiles and storms of state;
Torn from her throne, her country and her child,
And cast an exiled monarch on this wild,
She here was taught, what youthful beauty ne'er,
While seated on a throne had deigned to hear;
To say, submissive at the closing scene,
"'Tis well that I have thus afflicted been;"
Then calmly on the block, in faith, resign
Three heart-corrupting crowns for one divine-
Reader, the ways of God are not like thine.

* Transactions of the Hunter Archaeological Society, Vol 6.

Ribbledin. from The Christening
by Ebenezer Elliott[*]

The deeply wooded valleys of the Rivelin and the tumbling brooks that feed it, especially Wyming Brook, have long been popular for excursions from the city. This area was celebrated in verse most famously by Elliott, who christened it 'Ribbledin' as follows in his poem *The Christening*. He seems to capture some of the timeless nature of the place.

>No name hast thou, lone streamlet,
>   That marriest Rivelin;
>Here if a bard may christen thee,
>   I'll call thee Ribbeldin.
>Here, where first murmurings from thine urn,
>   Thy voice deep joy expresses,
>And down the rocks like music flows,
>   The wildness of thy tresses.

>   Dim world of sleeping mosses!
>   A hundred years ago
>   Yon hoary-headed holly tree
>   Beheld thy streamlet flow;
>   See how he bends him down to hear,
>   The tune that ceases never!
>   Old as the rocks, wild stream, he seams,
>   While thou art young for ever.

[*] Quoted in Pawson and Brailsford's 'Illustrated Guide to Sheffield', 1862.

My Native Rivelin   by Henry Waterfall, 1880*

s beautiful as the spot is it has inspired some pretty lamentable verses. The following offering from Henry Waterfall must be one of the poorest!

VIEW OF THE VALLEY OF THE RIVELIN, FROM TOUGH WOOD.

It is thy stream so fair I see
The highest source of joy to me-
It fills my heart to think of thee,
    My native Rivelin.

I hear the lambs' uncasing bleather
Joyful in the summer weather,
Playful on thy cliffs of heather,
    My native Rivelin.

Beneath thy beech and birken shade
The wearied heifer's resting laid,
Contented in the grassy glade.
    My native Rivelin.

* 'Rivelin Rhymes', Henry Waterfall, 1880.

The fly's the only living thing
That steadies on its gauzy wing,
And now and then it takes a fling,
    My native Rivelin.

View in Endcliffe Wood by W. Nicholson, 1862.

Thy silver streams their pride abate,
And country boys together prate
Paddling in thy half-dried gait,
    My native Rivelin.

But venting here my bosom's swell
Thy flying hour forbids me dwell,
And I must part with thee-Farewell!
    My native Rivelin.

The Old Home by the Don   by E. Darbyshire, 1885.*

Sheffield From the Attercliffe Road, E. Blore, in Hunter's Hallamshire, 1819.

I dream of my childhood, of days long since gone,
And once more I see my old house by the Don;
Its pretty embankments, and rails white as snow,
Come back with the memory of long, long ago.
The river, like silver, is bounding along,
And sweetest bird-music is swelling its song;
And lovely as ever sweet wild flowers grow,
That gladdened our young hearts so long, long ago.

In my dream, the old schoolhouse and scholars have come,
The lads and the lasses, all frolic and fun,
Down to the riverside romping we go.
But where are they gone since that long, long ago?
Some born to soldiers now peacefully sleep-
Some born to sailors are berthed in the deep;
And there's a sweet-voiced angel, I know,
Pleads for me in heaven, I loved long ago.

The old cot is there still, the river glides on,
But the birds, the flowers and the white rails are gone.
And o'er its dark waters red furnaces glow,
Where grew linnet bushes so long, long ago.
And man, like everything nature hath made,
All promise in springtime, in autumn must fade;
Here I am drooping, with hair white as snow,
And naught but a dream seems the long, long ago.

* 'Ballads, Poems & Recitations' by E.Darbyshire, Sheffield, 1885.

City of Steel

Author unknown, about 1980

Pouring Crucible Steel at Cammel's, 1870s.

It is not surprising that the 1980s prompted such an outpouring of verses similar to this one by ordinary working people as, with the dramatic demise of the steel industry whereby some 80,000 jobs were lost in the city over the decade, there was not much to look forward to for many older people, but much material for reminiscence.

The muscle, the brain, the blood of our sons,
Has gone into cutlery, bridges and guns,
Their nose to the grindstone, their back to the wheel,
The strong men of Sheffield; the city of steel.

When Sheffield was young they were forging the blades,
Of Templars in armour, all on the crusades,
They were hardened with toil, they were tempered with sweat,
And there's no finer steel in the world even yet!

The sons of the soil needed tools for their trade,
The ploughshare, the billhook, the sickle, the spade.
They were born in the furnace, baptised in the Don,
And the tools live today, though their makers have gone.

The working of pewter, of silver and gold,
Passed down generations from craftsmen of old,
Graced many a palace and mansion so fine,
With magic of symmetry, beauty of line.

In old Alamo a century ago,
Jim Bowie was famous, as well you must know.
The knives that he used in the old USA.
Are the same knives we're making in Sheffield today.

The Knife Grinders; Postcard from Sheffield, 1904.

The great war was on us, they took all our sons,
But those that are left made the shells and the guns.
Until armistice came and we counted the lives,
Then went back to making our forks and our knives.

World War II came, we were ready again,
With jets and with rockets, with tanks and with men,
Till the guns were struck dumb and the tyrants struck down,
Then Sheffield once more was a cutlery town.

Recession is biting, and increasing still,
Redundancies, bankruptcies, run of the mill,
But in spite of what many Job's Comforters feel,
'Old Sheff' will once more be the City of Steel.

The Contrast Or Improvements of Sheffield
by James Wills 1827

Will's poem is the most extraordinary piece of doggerel writing in Sheffield's history, quoted by every historian of the city's early nineteenth century. Wills, as will be obvious, was not a poet by trade, but a tailor. I have not reproduced the whole poem, which rambles on through many diversions over its twenty odd pages, only extracts which relate to some landmark or feature recognisable in the modern city. Quite why Wills felt himself up to the task of condensing the previous forty years of the town's development into verse is a mystery considering his evident lack of mastery of the medium. The content is, however, self-explanatory and useful in filling in some small gaps in our knowledge of the town that are not recorded elsewhere. The line 'The Gas-works most glorious!' must surely go down as one of the most unlikely lines of English poetry!

South East View of Sheffield, William Ibbett, 1856.

Ye Vet'rans of Sheffield, with intellects bright,
Whose memorys are good, may remember the sight
Of the streets, and the buildings, for sixty years past,
And with pleasure behold them improving-at last!

Take a view of the Town Hall, when near the Old Church,
And Sam Willerby's parlour,* his favourite lurch,
In which was the lobby, he frequently said,
"Have you clean'd out my parlour and made up my bed?"
A lodging which often he gained for his deeds,
By pilfering and stealing good things for his needs.

* Sam Willerby was evidently such a regular resident of the town lock-up, which occupied a space below the Town Hall, that Wills is able to refer to the gaol as his 'parlour'.

Proceed then up Church-Lane, that poor narrow place,
With wood buildings projecting! 'twas quite a disgrace,
The roofs nearly meeting, a dark dreary street,
Might justly be styled 'the robbers retreat';

Where shops were so darken'd for want of true light,
Appear'd quite at noontide, as though it were night;
For now what improvement is made in Church-Lane,
Fine shops for each tradesman whereby he may gain.

The Barker's Pool noted for nuisance indeed,
Green over with venom, where insects did breed,
And forming a square, with large gates in the wall,
Where the Rev. Charles Wesley to sinners did call.

From thence Virgin's Walk, now called West Parade,
A school for poor girls here is amply display'd;
In which large endowment poor orphans we find,
Who have *here* found a shelter from life's stormy wind.
Whose kind benefactors do amply provide
For their temporal wants, with instruction beside;
'Tis here they are taught both to knit and to sew,
To tread in the paths pure virtue doth shew.
The poor widow's heart has oft leaped for joy
To see her poor orphans this blessing enjoy:
What honour to Sheffield, and all who subscribe,
Yet the glory of God we must always ascribe.

You may form in your fancy a stile which once stood,
Near the little Grape Tavern, and made up of wood,
On the side of a field, then belonging to Hicks,
Where the children, at that time, have gather'd the sticks,
'Twas called Hicks-Stile-Field, and where corn oft has grown,
But Paradise Row when the stile was took down.

Many years it continued with only one row,
But now 'tis a beautiful square you know,*
With a Freemason's lodge, and flights of stone stairs,
And under it houses for various wares.
This square on the hill is a market for pots,
Which are sold, some by odd ones, others in lots.
A column in centre, with lamp of pure gas,
That lights all the square and he people who pass.

Near the silk draper's shop, (now the fruit market,) stood
The Shambles, most dismal, were then made out of wood:
The sheds almost closing, amain,
Form'd an archway for customers, out of the rain;
Down the centre, a channel, the filth to convey;
And some lighted candles, almost at mid-day.
But now 'tis commodious, and forms a good square,
With abundance of fruit and potatoes sold there.

* Referring to Paradise Square.

The Mechanics Institute

In Surrey-street, fronting down Eyre street, you find
A fine spacious building of the most superb kind,
Styled the Music Hall-famous for concerts and balls,
And decorative paintings on lofts and the walls.
For art and fine workmanship, who can excel?
Within and without is completed so well.

The Gas-works most glorious! They e'er should produce
Such a wonderful light for the township to use,
From a thing the most simple! The smoke of a coal-
To give such a brilliant light to the whole;
While those twinkling things which our ancestors had,
Made of cotton and oil, the effects must be bad;
Yet with all their good sense-still did none of them know,
How to light streets with gas lamps, as we have them now.

Urban Inflation   by Andrew Gregory, 1989

Sheffield is a city
without a zoo
though it has a grand town hall
and two football stadiums
and three police stations
somewhere

Sheffield is a city
sat on four small rivers
and a slightly larger one called the Don
a place that can boast five Shakespeares
serving as many lagers
and beers
and six galleries
(two still on the drawing board)

Sheffield is a city
like Rome
built on seven windy hills
a city with nine letters to its name
home to thirty different races
speaking sixty different tongues
in business big and small
a mint of money-making schemes
sending four thousand kids
to college
                    (a thousand more to gaol)

Sheffield is a city
where even now
twenty thousand are engaged in silent prayer
thirty thousand sighing love
forty shedding tear
city of half a million people
and one hundred million blades of grass
drenched by one billion drops of rain
shined on at night
by over two billion stars

The Beauty of Sheffield Plate
by L. du Garde Peach, 1948*

Contents of Display Cabinet, Walter Tricket's, Trippet Lane, 1980.

In ancient Sheffield by the Don,
Men wrought in steel in ages gone;
Till beauty from the valley sped,
    And trees were dead:

And no birds sang, where song had been,
And riven air put off the green
Of English fields and pastures rare,
    In black despair.

The sounds of rural life were stilled,
And in their stead the valley filled
With noise of anvil, forge and wheel,
    Until the steel

Entered the very souls of men:
And beauty no more dreamed again
Whence loveliness had passed and gone,
    Beside the Don.

Yet beauty stayed the hand of time,
And mid the ugliness and grime
Of iron and steel, it blossomed there
    In silver rare:

And hands long used to forge and press,
Fashioned to new found loveliness
The silvered copper, finely fused,
    Of Sheffield used.

Electro-Plate on Nickel Silver
Page from Harrison's Illustrated Catalogue, 1904.

*One of the poems from 'The Sheffield Pageant of Production' performed in front of Princess Margaret at the City Hall in November 1948.

An Edwardian Sunday, Broomhill, Sheffield
by John Betjeman, 1960[*]

Make way for the master! I don't know how much time Betjeman spent in Sheffield, rambling round the streets of middle-class Victorian villas in Broomhill but clearly he was in his element.

The Mount, Broomhill

High dormers are rising
So sharp and surprising,
And ponticum edges
The driveways of gravel;
Stone houses from ledges
Look down on ravines.
The vision can travel
From gable to gable,
Italianate mansion
And turreted stable,
A sylvan expansion
So varied and jolly
Where laurel and holly
Comingle their greens.

---

[*] Reproduced here by permission of John Murray, from John Betjeman's 'Collected Poems', Third Edition 1970.

Serene on a Sunday
The sun glitters hotly
O'er mills that on Monday
With engines will hum.
By tramway excursion
To Dore and to Totley
In search of diversion
The millworkers come;
But in our arboreta
The sounds are discreeter-
The worshippers wending
To welcoming chapel,
Companioned or lone;
And in a pew there
See loveliness lean,
As Eve shows her apple
Through rich bombazine:
What love is born new there
In blushing eighteen!

Your prospects will please her,
The iron-king's daughter,
Up here on Broomhill:
Strange Hallamshire, County
Of dearth and of bounty,
Of brown tumbling water
And furnace and mill.
You own Ebenezer
Looks down from his height
On back street and alley
And chemical valley
Laid out in the light;
On ugly and pretty
Where industry thrives
In this hill-shadowed city
Of razors and knives.

Regeneration   by Hazel Clarke, 1995

The pride which is so strongly expressed in poems of the early twentieth century has been replaced since the 1980s by a bewildered and bitter consternation at the turn of events which have so suddenly ripped the heart out of the city.

>Throughout the world Sheffield was steel,
>   Synonymous with smoke and grime
>Now steel is gone, and in its place
>   Are trees and shops and leisure time.

The Demolition of Viners' Broomhall Factory, 1985.
(Photo: Peter Machan)

>Where stood East Hecla's mighty works,
>   Turning out arms for Empire's wars,
>Stands Meadowhall, with parking space
>   For coaches and twelve thousand cars.

>Where are the fifty thousand jobs
>   That disappeared in one decade?
>Gone, with the city's proud, smug boast,
>   "It must be good, it's Sheffield made!"

The asset strippers took control,
    Their deity the rising pound.
Careless of jobs and ruined lives,
    They razed the East End to the ground.

And then a new regime sprang up,
    An Oasis of enterprise,
With jobs for trainees straight from school,
    This shoppers' dream of Paradise.

Which would we Sheffielders prefer?
    Supplying steel for cars and tanks
Or make the valley of the Don
    A leisure world of shops and banks?

Crucible Steel Melters, Meadowhall.
How many shoppers appreciate the irony of this superb sculpture,
standing as it does on the site of Hadfield's great steelworks?

Sheffield from 'In our Hands'
by Andrew Gregory, 1989

In the late 1980s the city was still reeling from the effects of the demise of its traditional heavy steel industry and the consequent loss of thousands of jobs. 'Regeneration' was the watchword but the strong sense of communal pride in being a world centre of production has proved impossible to recreate.

Sheffield once proud city
back-bone of empire and proud
empire's home
and died

While above your head
the crippled god of industry
Vulcan stoops down on town hall
stumbling

Leaving faces heavy
with a need for more
for something more
inside

Sheffield, Farewell! by E. Darbyshire, 1885

As someone who left Sheffield to go to college in Hull in the late 1960s I well remember the train journey through the east-end glow of the steelworks, especially Brown Bayley's and the familiarity of the sulphur smell welcoming me home again for the holidays.

Old Sheffield, my birthplace, I'm leaving behind me,
Her forest of chimneys now fades from my view;
I would not desert her, but fortune unkindly,
Tells me in tears, I must bid her adieu.
Lonely I go to the land of the stranger,
Faithfully trusting that fate may prove kind;
Fearless I feel, I shall brave every danger,
Yet sigh for the dear ones I'm leaving behind.

The city of sulphur that strangers hath found thee,
And black as thy smoke were the tales that they told;
Had they but climbed on the hills that surround thee,
They'd know thy black mantles have trimmings of gold.
Here are thine outskirts, oh what could be fairer?
These sweet hills and dales know no factory din;
While cottage and villa, and palace of splendour,
All speak of the home-joys that labour must win.

How full is my heart as I look thro' the window,
While, round the hillside, the train rushes on
Past the green fields, where the sons of hard labour,
Are meeting for pleasure their day's work is done.
Oh! Play on, dear friends, in cricket and football,
Sweet be your sport in the meadow and dell;
One, who has joined you, now bids you goodnight all;
One, who still loves you, now bids you farewell.

Moments in Time

Inscription at Sheffield Castle   14th Century

This inscription was reputedly discovered on a large, flat stone in the course of the demolition of the castle, although the story may be purely apocryphal since no trace of such a stone now seems to exist. It was from about 1280 that Thomas de Furnival, lord of the manor, set about the rebuilding of the castle into the very strongly fortified position that it became.

> I, LORD FURNIVAL,
> I BUILT THIS CASTLE HALL,
> AND UNDER THIS WALL
> WITHIN THIS TOMB WAS MY BURIAL.

from Sheffield Castle　　　by Francis Buchanan, 1882*

The recent excavations on the site of the castle give a refreshing relevance to this poem. There must be many a Sheffielder who, like the poet, has on occasion regretted both Cromwell's order that the castle must be 'slighted' following the civil war and the apparent thoroughness with which the operation was carried out. What a tourist attraction it would have been today!

> I cannot hail thee, tho' thou liv'st in story,-
>   They turrets and foundations all are gone,
> And nought is left to indicate thy glory
>   But old tradition and the beam of song.
>
> Spectre of time! Where are thy relics resting?
>   Where are the battlements and lordly hall?
> Nor vestige here, nor stone with noble crest in,
>   Nor remnant of a buttress or a wall.
>
> No effigy supreme, however broken,
>   No tottering gable in the sunlit glow,
> No grey remembrance that would be a token
>   To mark us back to ages long ago.
>
> No doubt thou look'd quite brave when thou existed,
>   And frowned defiance to the hills around;
> If thou the commonwealth had not resisted,
>   Thou might'st have still been standin on the ground.
>
> Thou might'st have been looking, grim and hoary,
>   Down on these busy thoroughfares below;
> A mould'ring moral to the ancient story
>   That castles, men, and all, are dust-you know.

* From 'Sparks from Sheffield Smoke', a series of local and other poems.

Ah! Thou would'st startle now in sheer amazement,
    If thou could'st only have one transient gleam,
'Twould make thee shake from bartisan to basement,
    And fancy all this hubbub was a dream.

The whirligigs of time and men and manners
    Have very nearly sent us all ajee,
Grim science now evolves his steamy banners,
    And on thy dust he crests his chivalry.

'Tis like a pantomimic transformation-
    The Sheffield of thy days-the Sheffield now,
Thy hamlet-town has grown a little nation,
    And time wreaths chaplets still upon its brow.

Sheffield Manor by Francis Buchanan, 1882

The passage of time has certainly not dealt kindly to most of Sheffield's important historic buildings. The Castle was destroyed and the Manor Lodge, that splendid Tudor manor house built by the 4th Earl of Shrewsbury in the middle of the deer park, began to decay early in the 17th century when the Dukes of Norfolk became Lords of the Manor, fulfilling their role largely as absentees. The manor house had great claims to fame in its celebrated visitors for Cardinal Wolsey stayed here for a short time on his final journey only a few days before his death, and Mary Queen of Scots wiled away parts of her fourteen years stay in Sheffield here. As it fell into a gradual state of disrepair part of the site became a public house, called the Norfolk Arms, part was used as a pottery and part was excavated for coal, all of which explains some of the references in this atmospheric poem.

Stop, for the ground is holy here;
Tread softly o'er this eminence,
Where time hath almost driven hence
The beauties I revere.

Sad memory contemplates the past,
And Fancy sighs for lost romance;
For demolition's grim advance
Hath wrinkled with its blast.

Here stood the Talbots' princely piles,
And in their paths the deer and hare
Heard the nightingale's sweet tune;
And the pool, at midnight there,
Imaged the brightness of the moon
Now a black pit defiles.

Here Mary sat, her wistful eye
Out-gazing o'er the broad expanse,
Watching the dark cloud-shadows dance
Across the sunny woods below;
Poor Queen, thou dreamt of future woe,
In thy captivity.

Now the Castalian spring is gone,
And gone are the Castalides,
And Fancy groans her vain distress;
The great oak trees and elms are dead,
And where the grand old chestnuts spread,
'Tis now a muddy lane instead,
Where beauty is unknown.

Romantic Fancy images
The buried past of other days,
(Like Endor's witch) her spells upraise;
She reconstructs the Manor-hall,
Where the dejected Cardinal
Mourned greatness that was his.

She fires the yule-log in the grate,
She spreads the board with haunch and loin,
And sparkles rimmers of red wine,
As knight and squire and ladye gay,
Swell music to the roundelay,
Nor miss the beggar at the gate.

She stimulates the stirring dance,
Where this old hybrid chaos stands;
And here, brave fingers pressed fair hands,
And lips breathed softly in the ear,
Where now a bumpkin sells his beer;
And where hung tapestries of grace,
The miner hath a dwelling place;
Grim craft usurps old elegance.

Steam Power   by Ebenezer Elliott*

In this piece Elliott leads an imaginary blind friend, Andrew Turner, to witness the transformation that the introduction of steam power is bringing to the town. The tone of this poem is especially interesting from a poet that we associate with rural eulogies.

> Come blind Andrew Turner! Link in mine
> Thy time-tired arm, and cross the town with me;
> For there are wonders mightier far than thine;
> Watt! and his million-feeding enginery!
> Steam-miracles of semi-deity!
> Thou can'st not see, from chimneys tall, the smoky cloud aspire;
> But thou can'st hear the unwearied crash and roar
> Of iron powers, that urged by restless fire,
> Toil ceaseless, day and night, yet never tire
> Or say to greedy men, "Thou dost amiss".
> Oh, there is glorious harmony in this
> Tempestuous music of the giant, Steam,
> Commingling growl and roar, and stamp, and hiss,
> With flame and darkness! Like a Cyclop's dream.

Sheffield at Night by Gordon Home in Yorshire by G. Home, 1908.

* Quoted in 'The Power of Steam' by Asa Briggs, 1982.

Norfolk Street Riots   by Joseph Mather, 1795

This song, one of Mather's most celebrated, relates to a riot which took place in Norfolk Street on August 4th, 1795. Being only a few years after the French Revolution, the national authorities were wary of the disrespectful attitudes of the citizens of the rapidly-growing industrial towns, and in Sheffield a regiment had recently been raised to ensure that order was maintained. Tensions were apparently running high when a trivial incident, a pay dispute amongst some of the privates, turned into a minor affray and a crowd gathered. Colonel Athorpe, the commanding officer, was summoned from Wentworth Woodhouse where he had been dining (and, presumably, wining) with Earl Fitzwilliam. The Riot Act was read but when the people took little heed of the red-faced colonel's orders to disperse Athorpe plunged about on his horse, slashing with his sword. An order was given to fire on the confused and frightened crowd. Two were killed and several wounded. Montgomery, writing about the event in his paper 'The Iris' took a very similar view to the one expressed by Mather in this song and was prosecuted for the libel on Colonel Athorpe, was found guilty and served six months in York Castle. Mather, despite his language being far less guarded, escaped prosecution; on this occasion.

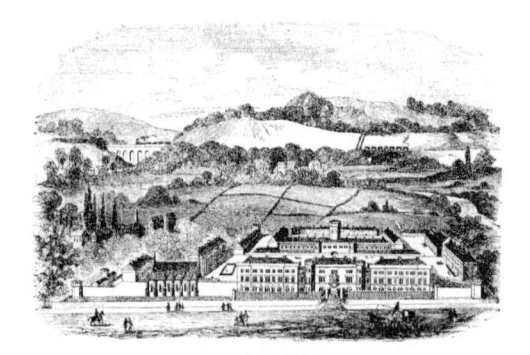

The New Barracks, built as a result of the unrest in the early nineteenth century.

Corruption tells me homicide
Is wilful murder justified,
A striking precedent was tried
   In August 'ninety-five,

When armed assassins dressed in blue
Most wantonly their townsmen slew,
And magistrates and juries too
    At murder did connive.

I saw the tragic scene commence;
A madman drunk, without offence
Drew out his sword in false pretence,
    And wounded some more wise;
Defenceless boys he chased about,
The timid cried, the bold did shout,
Which brought the curious no doubt
    To see what meant the noise.

'Twas manifest in the event
That what the bloody tyrant meant
Was murder without precedent,
    Though by injustice screened.
The 'Courant' may her columns swell,
Designing men may falsehoods tell,
Not all the powers of earth and hell
    Can justify the fiend.

This armed banditti, filled with spleen,
At his command, like bloodhounds keen,
In fine, to crown the horrid scene,
    A shower of bullets fired.
The consequence was deep disress,
More widows, and more fatherless,
The devil blushed and did confess
    'Twas more than *he* required.

Corruption cried, 'for this exploit
His worship shall be made a knight,
I hold his conduct just and right,
    And think him all divine.'
Oppression need not fear alarms,
Since tyranny has got such swarms
Of gallant heroes bearing arms,
    To butcher grunting swine.

Ye wanton coxcombs, fops and fools,
Aristocratic dupes and tools,
Subject yourselves to better rules,
    And cast away that badge.
Remember on a future day
Corruption must be done away,
Then what will you presume to say
    When truth shall be your judge?

The Invitation   by Joseph Senior, 1882

*The Statue of Elliott in its original position in the Market Place.
It now stands in Weston Park.*

Come, let us raise a monument,
Famed Elliott's worth to spread,
Who laboured hard through life to feed
The poor with 'untaxed bread;'
And be it to posterity,
While it shall grace the earth,
A censure to the Tyrant,
A spur to honest worth.

Impromptu, Written on the Opening of Firth Park by E. Darbyshire, 1875.

The noble Mayor, whose gift to Sheffield this poem celebrates, is Mark Firth, the owner of the Norfolk Steel works, whose fine home, Oakbrook, still stands at Ranmoor. It is unusual to find two poems written to celebrate the same occasion but the first Royal visit to Sheffield since the confinement of Mary Queen of Scots was clearly an event worthy of note.

Entrance to Firth Park, 1875

Oh let our hill re-echo,
While thousands breathe the prayer,
God bless the Prince and Princess;
God bless our noble Mayor.
The royal pair of England
With pleasure lead the van,
Nor blush to make acquaintance
With Nature's nobleman.
He is the best of princes
Who plays a princely part,
The noblest of the noble,
Who owns a noble heart.
We've seen its finest feeling,
Engraven on Ranmoor;
And felt its kindly beating,
Have they, the old and poor.

When years have clothed in history,
>   The opening of our park,
It will not be forgotten
>   Who played the leading part.
And tho' our Prince and Princess,
>   Their page in history claim;
Our noble mayor and mayoress
>   Will honoured be the same.

*Mark Firth 1819-1880, Master Cutler,
Lord Mayor and founder of the Norfolk Steel Works.*

from The Welcome of the Men of Hallamshire to the Prince and Princess of Wales
by John Hall, August 1875.*

To England's future king
   And Denmark's daughter fair-
The brightest gem by far
   That king will ever wear-
The sturdy Vulcan race,
   The Cyclops of the day-
The men of terrible renown-
   Of Sheffield's ill-reputed town,
Their loyal homage pay!

Three hundred years have passed
   Since Royal footsteps trod
Yon ancient castle court
   Where Shrewsbury's fortress stood;
And then, a captive Queen,
   Unfortunate as fair,
Whose only welcome was the sound
   Of tramping sentinels around,
Guarding with jealous care.

* From 'Thoughts and sketches in verse' by John Hall ('J.H.J') Sheffield 1891.

And the proud Lord of Hallam,
    The Norfolk of today,-
Heir of the ancient Manor
    Where Shrewsbury held sway,
Now joins his loyal tenants,
    And opens wide his gate,
To give a welcome fit and meet
    His future sovereign to greet
With honourable state!

Long live the generous host!
    Whose enterprising soul
Hath gained the town this honour
    And given a park withal!
And long may Sheffield Vulcans
    Enjoy the noble boon;
And future generations rise
    To emulate the enterprise
Of Hallam's princely son!

The Triumphal Arch built for the occasion on Lady's Bridge

A Street Scene by William Dowsing, 1910*

William Dowsing stands out as a writer quite apart from the general run of doggerel merchants represented here as an intellectual who struggled to achieve a mastery of writing poems in the sonnet form. His destitute family finished up in Sheffield Workhouse in the 1870s, having tramped around the country following his father's death. He studied in the evenings whilst working at Vickers steelworks where his talent was recognised by the manager who arranged to have his work published. Three collections of the thousands that he wrote were published but were not a commercial success, and he died in poverty in 1954.

'Mid heavy smoke wreaths black as witchery
  (The liberated imps of unknown days,)
'Mid furnace flames that shoot volcanic rays
  (The sunbeams of a lost eternity,)
A street piano, plethoric with harmony,
  Is tinkling forth its iterating lays;
And happy children, lithe as forest fays,
Around the tinnient organ trip with glee.
Red flames illuminate the children now,
Huge flames like monstrous living blossomings
  That belch from chimneys hidden in the night:
Yet on they dance within the lurid glow
Like splendid fairies dressed in magic light,
  Sweet music in their hearts and kindred things.

* From 'Sheffield Viquettes', a series of sonnets by William Dowsing, Sheffield 1910.

Opening of the New Town Hall   21st May, 1897*

This comes from the souvenir programme of the jubilee of the opening of the town hall printed in May 1947. The opening of the Town Hall in 1897 was a very significant moment for Sheffield in more ways than one, for it was the first time that a reigning monarch had ever visited the city. The nine foot high 'brazen figure' of Vulcan still stands proud over the modern city centre although as this early print of the proposed Town Hall shows, a very different figure was originally planned. I can't help feeling that this strange poem does not accurately express the sentiments intended by the city fathers at this momentous occasion.

> A stately pile is raised, new civic home
> Of those who shape the city's destiny,
> And on the topmost pinnacle shall stand
> The brazen figure of a heathen god.
> Now is the scene set for a fitting act
> Which crowns a century of civic state.
> Victoria of England, sixty years a Queen,
> Comes to the city.

56

The Old Queen's Visit. from - 'A Song of Welcome.'
by G.C. Moore, 1897

This ode comes from one of the official souvenir programmes sold on the occasion of the visit by Queen Victoria to open the Town Hall in May 1897. The city came to a standstill as thousands turned out to cheer the first visit by a ruling sovereign. In the event the old Queen spent only two hours here and never alighted from her carriage during the whole visit!

Ring, ye bells, till ye rock your steeples!
Flaunt, ye flags, on the breeze of May!
Never in all our city's story
Rose the sun on a prouder day!

Forge and mart shall today be idle;
Strife and party shall hush their call;
She is among us who binds us like brothers;
Welcome Her, welcome Her, Mother of all!

Three-score years hah the hawthorn whitened,
Three-score times hath the wood grown green,
Since that dawn when a royal maiden
Heard the message "We hail thee Queen."

Glist'ning eyed, but with heart undaunted,
True to duty, She stretched her hand,
Girl in years but a Queen in daring,
Grasped the sceptre to rule Her land.

Crushed by sorrow, she clung to duty,
Toiled still more for Her People's weal,
Lived to suffer with those who suffer,-
"I have borne it and I can feel."

Ours the love to-day that greets Her,
Ours, whose labours of head and hand,
Rapid brain and strenuous muscle
Forge the armour that fends Her land.

Ring, ye bells, till ye rock your steeples!
Fling your peals on the breeze of May!
England's Mother shall hear your music;
When had ye ever so proud a day?

The Statue of Queen Victoria, now in Endcliffe Park

Sir Henry Coward, Mus.D., M.A. - Our Great Conductor.
By Ellen Styring.

Sir Henry Coward, who lived at Sharrow Head, was Sheffield's greatest chorus master. He was a familiar figure on the podium in front of the Sheffield Choral Union and on a platform conducting one of the great Whit sings in the park. His greatest triumph, however, was undoubtedly the occasion on which he conducted the nine bands and massive children's choir in front of Queen Victoria when she rode through Norfolk Park following the opening of the Town Hall in 1897.

> Of good Sir Henry here we sing,
> A worthy tribute let us bring
>   To honour his great name.
> For sixty years our Chorus King,
> His famous choirs triumphant sing,
>   And glory crowns their fame.
>
> From humble life began his day,
> But perseverance won the way
>   For music's sheer delight.
> In workshop or in teacher's role,
> With urge of genius in his soul
>   A vision held his sight.
>
> His far-famed Sheffield Festivals
> Enraptured melodies forthtell,
>   Sublime and true and free.
> Transfused on air, the strains we hear,
> Led by a youthful veteran peer
>   In glorious harmony.
>
> His choir has travelled far and wide,
> And on his wisdom we relied
>   To spread our City's name.
> Great laurels they have truly won
> Through their conductor, Sheffield's son
>   Long live his world-wide fame.

Henry Coward Conducting the Children's Choir in Norfolk Park.

A Street March of the Sheffield Boy's Brigade
by Ebenezer Downing, 1906

Empire Day Pageant, Bramall Lane, 1906 in which 10,000 children took part.

What a chilling poem this is, not just because of its unpleasantly militaristic tone but because, considering its date, Downing must have been watching many of the boys who were to be recruited into the Sheffield City Battalion of the Yorkshire and Lancashire regiment which was mown down on the morning of July 1st 1916 in the battle of the Somme. 'T'Stooaker' could never have known what foreboding was hinted at in his prophetic line 'learning war for war's alarms'.

    Here they come with a tap of drum,-
        Sheffield lads, Sheffield lads;-
    Every boy his mother's joy;-
        Sheffield lads;-
    One his 'sis' would love to kiss,-
        Sheffield lads, Sheffield lads;
    And how proud they make their dads,-
        Bless the lads.
    Stepping out with limbs so stout,-
        Sheffield lads, Sheffield lads;-
    Rank on rank of faces frank,-
        Sheffield lads;

Learning arms for war's alarms,-
                Sheffield lads, Sheffield lads;
Up they come to help their dads,-
                Sheffield lads.
Now they pass, a swinging mass,-
                Sheffield lads, Sheffield lads;-
As they go their bugles blow,-
                Sheffield lads;
Rings the street with tramp of feet,-
                Sheffield lads, Sheffield lads;
And who wouldn't, with the dads,
                Bless the lads?

Cry From the City by C.A.Renshaw, 1916[*]

It was only when I had virtually completed compiling this anthology that I discovered the vast collection of poems of both the World Wars written by Sheffield's very own war poet. Miss C.A. Renshaw was a poet of some distinction, her work having been published in the Poetry Review[**]. She regularly contributed pieces to the Sheffield Telegraph and her monthly contributions were a feature of each publication of 'All Clear', the magazine of the ARP Wardens from 1940 to 1945. The harsh jingoism of these verses, however, especially those written in the later years, strikes a jarring chord today, despite their poetic merit. Many of her poems skilfully parody other writers such as Tennyson and Kipling. This beautiful poem is the only real love poem in this collection. Was this written from tragic personal experience, I wonder?

>'Cushla! cushla! 'cushla! 'tis the soul of you I'm wanting,
>Here in dingy Sheffield with its smoke-dark streets.
>You are of the grass-ways where golden winds go slanting;
>You are of the ocean where the Great Heart beats.
>
>Here in smoky Sheffield there are labours without ending,
>Furnaces that throb and surge the whole night through.
>...You are of the pine-woods with silent payers ascending;
>All the little lanes of dusk are filled with you.
>
>'Cushla! cushla! 'cushla! When we watched the shadows falling,
>You and I together on the lone wide moors,
>Softly in the wind song, the heart of you was calling;
>Love was beating, beating on my heart's closed doors.
>
>You and I together with the windy dark around us,
>You and I together in a blue dream-mist!
>...Stars were born in strangeness, for urgent love had found us;
>All the world was breathless as we stooped and kissed.

* From 'England's Boys; A woman's War Poems', C.A.Renshaw, London, 1916.
** Poetry Review, Vol.8, 1917.

'Cushla! cushla! 'cushla! 'tis the heart of me that's sobbing
Here in lonely Sheffield with its sad grey skies.
Here is mighty Travail with its tireless engines throbbing.
…You are of the moorland where the low wind sighs!

You are just a hush of leaves-a bird-song in the may-field;
Just a quiet wood-way where the sun-beams rove;
Just the hint of glamour in the moon above the hay-field;
Just the breath of Beauty …for you brought me Love!

'Cushla! cushla! 'cushla! Will you never hear me calling,
Calling out in anguish for your dear white face?
Will you never come again and watch the shadows falling,
You and I together in a dream-lit place?

First World War Re-enactment Soldiers, Norfolk Park, 2003.
(Photo: Peter Machan)

Cole's Corner — by Ebenezer Downing, 1906.

The 'Cole's Corner' referred to here is not in Barker's Pool but was at the bottom corner of Church Street, on the corner occupied by Cole's store until 1960. Right until the old shop was demolished this spot was the favourite rendezvous of anyone arranging to meet in the city centre, but after the corner lost its identity it also lost this function.

> Let me sing of the joys of Cole's Corner
>   On a Saturday morning in May;
> Let me tell Sheffield's lordliest scorner
>   There's a spot in old Sheffield that's gay
>
> As the morning wears on to eleven,
>   Fargate dons a livelier air,
> As if this was her one day in seven
>   To have of dear life a full share.

Cashiers have come up for the wages-
    Thatched houses are handy for lunch;
Schoolmasters, wise looking as sages,
    Are taking the air in a bunch.

Here's a filecutter, bundle on shoulder,
    An outworker going to 'weigh in';
A grinder, a cutler, a moulder,
    Looking round till it's time for the 'tin.'

Now sounds the 'hoot-toot' of the motor,
    With a rush the road-demon is here,
(And you wish he'd a less strident note, or
    A magistrate's summons to fear),

While swiftly, serenely and truly,
    Wheel many a carriage and pair,
Till ranged by the kerbstone they duly
    Await the return of the fair.

Musicians, reporters, directors,
    Boy messengers, postmen on round,
Are elbowing vicars and rectors-
    This is no Tommy Tiddler's ground.

Here, looking as fresh as the Graces,
    Sheffield's daughters so lightly flit by
With such charm in their motion and faces,
    You could fancy that heaven was nigh.

And now comes the maddening moment,
    The Parish Church clock's striking one;
We're just at the height of the foment,
    Let us mount on a car and be gone.

But it's oh! For a look at Cole's Corner
    On a Saturday morning in May;
And I'll tell Sheffield's haughtiest scorner
    There's a spot in old Sheffield that's gay.

Beatlemania   by Susan Alexander 1966*

The 'Fab Four' had not been together long when they played at the City Hall, and I don't think the staff there knew what they were in for! I regret not having had the foresight to buy a ticket for the concert but I well remember the girls in the class coming to school the next morning still flushed with the experience.

We went to the City Hall to see the Beatles.
We walked in.
There was an air of excitement.
The teenagers jumped up and down, impatient and restless,
The artists came on and disappeared.
We waited, we waited,
Oh! how we waited,
Impatiently tormented by the thought of our idols.
The minutes ticked by, they seemed like hours.
The names of "John", "Paul", "George", "Ringo"
Rang out in deafening tones,
The hall was in uproar,
We were crying and laughing,
Shouting and screaming,
Stamping and calling the names of our idols.
The place was boiling and steaming,
The temperature rising at the sound of each note.
Then, without warning, the lifeline was cut
And John, Paul, George, Ringo just vanished,
Like salt running out of a bag.
The light came on, the hall was emptying,
And we all came out with hearts sad and weary,
But bearing a memory of those fabulous four.

* From New Horizons, Myers Grove School Magazine 1966

Coal

by Hazel Clarke, 1990

What makes this Government lay waste
        Three hundred years of coal, that lies
Beneath our feet, when their decree
        Means Britain's coal industry dies?

Then thirty thousand miners told
        This callous way, their jobs would go.
There's no preamble, no warning,
        Does the last strike still rankle so?

Divide and rule's the strategy
        The miner's loyalties split in two,
A spent force with their power base gone
        What could their rival unions do?

Unprecedented the support
        That's given up and down the land,
Perhaps that means we've left behind
        Those selfish years to make this stand.

Pickets at Orgreave by J. 1987.

Oh! What a lovely summer,
Oh! What a long, long strike,
But if we have to go through it all again,
We would still stand up and fight.

Convoys of coke going from Orgreave,
Men standing side by side,
Women serving soup for them,
Watching lorries go by.

Rows and rows of men in blue,
Horses! Dogs! and truncheons too,
Hitting miners, they didn't care who.

How can we forget that sad, sad time,
Dads, sons and brothers who were on that picket line.
Memory will erase many things
As time goes by,
But in our hearts
What happened at Orgreave that day will never die.

I'm proud I married a miner,
I'm proud they're friends of mine,
You see I knew a host of them,
That were on that picket line.

Song for the Picket Lines   by Miner's Wife, 1984

Dad, the kettle's boiling,
Hey dad, what's the time?
Dad, where is our mother?
She's on the picket line.

Dad we want our dinner,
Dad we're nearly pined,
Dad where is our mother?
She's on the picket line.

Oh dad when this is over,
And we are feeling fine,
We'll always remember
That bloody picket line.

Dad, when we are grown up
And we're down the mine,
If the Union need us
We'll be on the picket line.

The Death of the Rag and Tag   by Ralph Thickett, 1973.

The 'Rag and Tag' market, properly called the Sheaf Open Market, was a remarkable survival; the last relic of the nineteenth century market undertakings which were purchased from the Duke of Norfolk in 1899. Much loved by Sheffielders, it had its own antiquated character and characters; the ancient woman with the weighing contraption, the pot sellers juggling piles of crockery and the quack medicine sellers and, as a small boy, Saturday wasn't complete without a visit to the cave-like hollow lined with cages of rabbits and small animals. This verse, composed, I assume by Ralph Thickett the butcher, was distributed to customers in its last weeks.

For years and years you've served us well,
    In summer and in winter;
With canvas tops and paraffin lamps,
    And stalls made all o' timber.

That's how it used to be, tha' knows,
    When my dad wor a lad,
A good day out it used to be,
    Just scrounging in our rag.

Ther isn't owt tha cudna get,
    From a barra to a brolly,
We've got more comics in our rag,
    Than tha'll ever see on't telly.

But progress ses it's got to go,
    And it makes me feel reight sad,
No screaming kids that's lost their mam,
    No purses pinched by Slippery Sam.

But now the time is getting near,
    When one and all will shed a tear
On't third of March the drums will roll,
    And progress and time will take their toll.

Sheaf 'Rag 'n Tag' Market, about 1930. The lady with the scales was still there when I was a lad!

Grime and Poverty

Sheffield by William Carpenter, 1877.

There is nothing nostalgic or romantic about this uncompromising view of the city, as Edward Carpenter looks down from the surrounding hills. Indeed his eye seems almost jaundiced and fails to find merit of any kind in what appears to be an appallingly ugly and harsh environment. This is a stranger's impression, a stranger who allows his preconceptions full reign. Anyone who knew pre-war Sheffield can attest to the truth of the filthy atmosphere and indeed until the early 1960s it was not unusual to venture out into the bright sunshine of a cold autumn morning and witness the valleys below filled with dense unhealthy smog like a swirling grey sea, the very sort of day that Carpenter apparently chose to visit the city. He was clearly familiar with some aspects of the town and its trades, for he paints a graphic picture of the worker hand-cutting files.

Where a spur of the moors runs forward into the great town,
And above the squalid bare steep streets, over a deserted quarry,
    the naked rock lifts itself into the light,
There, lifted above the smoke, I stood,
And below lay Sheffield.

The great wind blew over the world,
The sky overhead was serenest blue, and here and there a
    solitary white cloud scudded swiftly below it.
The great soft wind! How it blew in gusts as it would uproot
    the very rocks, eddying and whistling round the angles!
The great autumnal wind! bearing from the valley below
    clouds of paper and rubbish instead of dead leaves.

Yet the smoke still lay over Sheffield.
Sullenly it crawled and spread;
Round the bases of the tall chimneys, over the roofs of the
    houses, in waves - and the city was like a city of chimneys
    and spires rising out of a troubled sea -
From the windward side where the roads were shining wet with
    recent rain,
Right across the city, gathering, mounting, as it went,
To the eastward side where it stood high like a all, blotting the
    land beyond,
Sullenly it crawled and spread.

Dead leaden sound of forge-hammers,
Gaping mouths of chimneys,
Lumbering and rattling of huge drays through the streets,
Pallid faces moving to and fro in myriads,
The sun, so brilliant here, to those below like a red ball, just
    visible, hanging;
The drunkard reeling past; the file cutter humped over his
    bench, with ceaseless skill of chisel and hammer cutting his
    hundred thousand file teeth per day - lead-poison and
    paralysis slowly creeping through his frame;

The gaunt woman in the lens-grinding shop, preparing
      spectacle- glasses without end for the grindstone - in eager
      dumb mechanical haste, for her work is piecework;

Barefoot skin-diseased children picking the ash-heaps over,
      Sallow hollow-cheeked young men, prematurely aged ones,
The attic, the miserable garret under the defective roof,
The mattress on the floor, the few coals in the corner,
White jets of steam, long ribbons of black smoke,
Furnaces glaring through the nights, beams of lurid light
      thrown obliquely up through the smoke,
Nightworkers returning home wearied in the dismal dawn-
Ah! How long? How long?

And as I lift my eyes, lo! Across the great wearied throbbing
      city the far unblemished hills,
Hills of thick moss and heather,
Coming near in the clear light, in the recent rain yet shining,
And over them along the horizon moving, the gorgeous
      procession of shining clouds,
And beyond them, lo! In fancy, the sea and the shores of other
      lands,
And the great globe itself curving with its land and its sea and
      its clouds in supreme beauty among the stars.

The Old Canal. from Broughton Lane Bridge
by William Dowsing, 1910*

Bacon Street Bridge, Sheffield Canal. A. Morrow, 1884.

Amidst an avenue of haunting shades
    The old canal in ice-like dumbness sleeps,
    It stretches dimly into distant deeps-
The deeps of night's phantasmal shadow-glades.
And while the morning star's fresh brilliance fades,
    Smoke-dimmed coke-oven conflagration leaps
    Athwart the horizon, where, new born, peeps
The dawn through clouds that hang like dusky braids.
Dim railway signal-lights, gold, red and green,
    Scarce glint the train track curving out of sight;
    A coal barge, symbol of the ending night,
Awakes the calm canal from sleep serene;
And now street jets and every signal light
    Are lost, for morning's lamp has lit the scene.

* 'Sheffield Vignette, A Series of Sonnets' by William Dowsing, 1910.

Dirty Sheffield.

Poet unknown, early 19th century

In a fair country, stands a filthy town,
By bugs and butchers held in high renown;
Sheffield the Black - in ugliness supreme;
Yet ugly Sheffield is my dirty theme.
Where slowly down the vale a river runs,
Of dark complexion like its crooked sons;
Ah, luckless he, who in unhappy hour
Is doomed to walk our streets beneath the shower,
No friendly spout from the projecting eaves,
The copious tribute of the clouds receives,
But headlong from the roof, in sooty showers,
Prone on the hapless passenger it pours.
While on the moonless evenings, dark and damp,
Imprudent thrift denies the public lamp
And many a dunghill graces many a street.
Whole streams of rubbish and whole seas of mud;
With turnip tops, potato peelings join,
And to their cast garments, peas and beans combine,
Providing pigs and ducks with goodly cheer;
To pigs and ducks our streets are ever dear,
May no audacious scavenger presume to wield the rake,
the shovel or the broom!

From Hungry Forties

by 'T'Owd Hammer 1937

Aw'm sickened o' hearin'o't' 'gooid owd toimes'
Aw knew they wor nowt o't' sooart;
Ther wor verry few dollars, an' not many doimes,
An' monny a ramshackle cooat.

Peeak thissen dahn on t'grindle-cowk top,
An' hark while Aw tell thi a tale;
An't' next toime thah gooas for thi muther to t'shop,
Be glad thah can pay reight on t'nail.

The Tip

by William Dowsing

Digging for outcrop coal at Darnall during the 1912 coal strike.

Unwashed, unkempt, half clothed, half-shod, they stand
       Upon the squalid tip, early and late;
       Sad human derelicts of ruthless Fate,
Women and children, Poverty's own brand.
Out of this future workman's cottage land
       They rake scarce scrap that's bought at niggard rate,
       Or fuel for a seldom-heated grate,
To cook what sorts of food they can command,
Fluent with oaths, the carter comes along,
       Whilst these poor laughing-stocks of Fortune crowd
       Together for the wolfish strife;
And when the load is shot (all right and wrong
The devil take!) amid the screaming cloud
       They rake, reckless of God, or love - for life.

The File Hewer's Lamentation by Joseph Mather, 1780

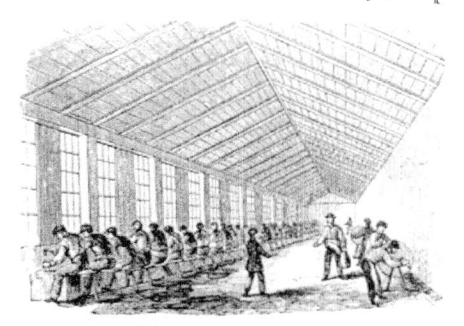

File Cutters Shop-W.Hall and Son, Alma Works, 1862

Ordained I was a beggar,
And have no cause for swagger;
It pierces like a dagger,
    To think I'm thus forlorn.
My trade and occupation
Was ground for lamentation,
Which makes me curse this station
    And wish I'd ne'er been born.

Of starving I am weary,
From June to January.
To nature it's contrary;
    This, I presume, is fact.
Although without a stammer
Our Nell exclaims I clam her,
I wield my six pound hammer
    'Till I'm grown round-backed.

As Negroes in Virginia
In Maryland or Guinea,
Like them I must continue
    To be both bought and sold.
While Negro ships are filling
I ne'er can save one shilling,
And must- which is more killing
    A pauper die when old.

Nickerpeckers Complaint at Government Regulations.*

There's to be two ventilators
In good order and repair;
Us 'at's short o' beef an' taters,
Has to fatten on fresh air.
An' for ivr'y bloomin' stiddie
There's so many cubic feet,
We'st ha' room to play at hiddie-
Us 'at isn't aat I' t' street!

*Quoted by J.S. Fletcher in 'The Story of English Towns, Sheffield, 1919.

Song of the Men on the Parish at Hollow Meadows
19th Century*

This verse was said to have been written by one of the paupers at the Workhouse at Hollow Meadows, high on the moorland above the Rivelin Valley. The 'Fox' refers to the Duke of Norfolk's keeper.

> There was a fox sat in his den,
> He sat to watch poor parish men;
> He sat where he had sat before
> To tent the bilberries on the moor.
> These Foxes they are very sly,
> And they are fond of bilberry pie;
> They can have rabbits and hares, and birds and fish,
> And all the dukes or lords could wish.
> These parish men they are poor sinners
> And can't have bilberry pie to their dinners.

Words of a Sheffield Street Song
early 19th Century

It appears that these words were based on fact, for in 1796 John Lees, a 'steel burner' led his wife by halter round her neck to the market place where he sold her to Samuel Hall, fellmonger, for sixpence.

> In Sheffield market, I declare,
> 'Tis true upon my life,
> A cotton spinner t'other day,
> By auction sold his wife.

---

* As recorded by Thomas Winder in 'T' Hefts 'an Blades O Shefvield', 1907.

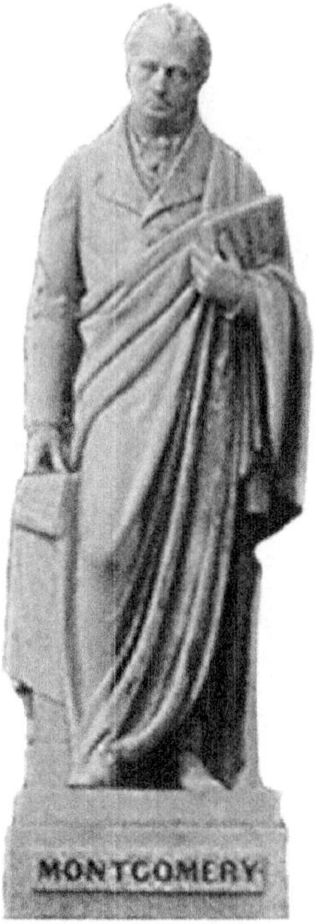
MONTGOMERY

A Working life

The Sheffield Cutler

by L. du Garde Peach, 1948

The Cutler, 1825

Since first from iron
The steel was made,
Since first man fashioned
Heft and blade;
Since man relied
On sword or knife,
To win his bread
Or guard his life;
By day the sparks have flown,
From steel upon the grinder's stone.

*Model of Grinder,
Simon Ogden, 1985.*

Extract from 'The Reeve's Tale',
Canterbury Tales
by Geoffrey Chaucer, 1387-92*

There is not an author of any book on Sheffield history that has resisted the temptation include this most famous earliest reference to Sheffield wares, and I am not to be the first. The miller in this tale is here described, and a most unprepossessing character he evidently is. We can conclude that whilst it is interesting to note that a reference to a Sheffield made knife, or 'thwittel', must have had a wide understanding amongst Chaucer's readers, the rough and ready nature of the miller would indicate that the town was not renowned for producing the most refined or highest quality articles.

The Canterbury Tales window, by Christopher Webb, in the Cathedral Chapter House. The miller is depicted at the top.

* Original and translation taken from Everyman edition of Canterbury Tales, ed. A.C. Cawley, 1958.

At Trumpygtoun, nat fer fro Canterbrigge,
Ther gooth a brook, and over that a brigge,
Upon the whiche brook ther stant a melle;
And this is verray sooth that I yow telle.
A Millere was ther dwellynge many a day.
As any pecok he was proud and gay.
Pipen he Konde and fisshe, and nettes beete,
And turne coppes, and well wrestle and sheete;
Ay by his belt he baar a long panade,
And of a swerd ful trenchant was the blade.
A jolly poppere baar he in his pouche;
There was no man, for peril, dorste hym touche.
A Sheffield thwittel baar he in his hose.
Round was his face, and camus was his nose;
As piled as an ape was his skulle.
He was a market-betere alte fulle.

In modern day English this would translate something as follows-

At Trumpington, near Cambridge,
There runs a brook, and over it there is a bridge.
On this brook there stands a mill,
And this is the truth that I now do tell.
A miller lived there many a day;
As any peacock he was proud and gay.
He could play the pipes, fish and mend the nets,
Turn wooden cups, wrestle and shoot well with a bow;
He always carried a large knife at his belt,
As well as a sharp sword.
A handsome dagger he carried in a pouch;
Not surprisingly, no one dared touch him.
A Sheffield knife he carried tucked into his sock.
He had a round face and a flat nose;
He was as bald as an ape.
At the market he was a swaggering nuisance.

Extract from
The Merry Travellers
anon, 1720*

Competition from London cutlers was fierce and they were not above employing the writing of verses to rubbish the Sheffield products. Maybe we should see this as a back-handed compliment!

A man called How of Southend town,
Made a knife of such renown,
If touched upon a stair or stone,
Will cut a sirloin to the bone,
And at one stroke, to human wonder,
Divide the stubborn joints asunder.

No Yorkshire carrier at a meal
Durst draw a Sheffield blade of steel,
And boast his cutting country bauble
If one of Hows adorns the table.
Their rustic tools are only fit
For rural poesies, void of wit,
And to divide fat pork or peasen,
Or cut down hooks in nutting season.

Brian Truelove, knifemaker of Greenhill, 1975.
(Photo: Peter Machan)

* Quoted by R.E. Leader in 'Sheffield in the Eighteenth Century', 1901

Buffer Girl　　　　　　　　　　by Margaret Morley, 1990

Regiments of girls and women spent their lives tediously buffing or polishing cutlery and silverware in the city centre factories; high quality bought at a shockingly high price.

> Our cutlery's created
> From Sheffield's finest steel,
> Its strength you can rely on
> To use at every meal.
> So many styles to choose from
> Of beautiful design
> To grace the finest table
> When friends are asked to dine.
> Made by Sheffield cutlers
> Whose skill is tried and true
> A craft learned through the centuries
> To bring the best to you.
> We create the finest tableware,
> Meet the highest of demands
> Making cutlery from Sheffield
> A joy to every hand.

Buffer Girls, Walter Tricket's, 1920s.

The Song of the City of Steel
by L. du Garde Peach, 1948

Tapping an Electric Arc Furnace, Steel, Peach and Tozer, 1948.
This melting shop has now become the attraction MAGNA.

We who tamed the fires that flamed,
    Harnessed to our will the power,
Learned of right the mastery
    In that fatal hour,
When combining fire and earth,
    Steel was brought to mighty birth.

May the blinding fires we tend,
    May the skill we proudly give,
Serve the centuries to come,
    That the world may live:
This is our prayer, that we may be
    Of those who build prosperity.

Louisin' Day   Traditional, 18th century

It was hardly surprising that on the day that a young apprentice, having served under the harsh regime of his master for seven years, was finally freed he would wish to celebrate, for this was his 'louisin' day'. The words speak for themselves. The celebration was the occasion for much drunkenness and rowdy behaviour and was finally put a stop to by the authorities

The Sheffield Cutler from George Walker's 'Costumes of Yorkshire', 1814.

This young man's health, an it shall gooa rahnd,
It shall gooa rahnd, it shall gooa rahnd;
This young man's health, and it shall gooa rahnd,
It shall gooa rahnd, hoi o!

Houd yer likker aboon er chin,
Aboon yer chin, aboon yer chin;
Houd yer likker aboon yer chin,
Aboon yer chin, hoi o!

Open yer mahth an let likker run in,
T'likker run in, t'likker run in;
Open yer mahth an let likker run in,
T'likker run in, hoi o!

O'l houd ya a crahn it's all gone dahn,
It's all gone dahn, its all gone dahn,
O'l houd ya a crahn it's all gone dahn,
It's ll gone gahn, hoi o!

Here's a health to he, that is nah set free,
Which once as a 'prentice bahnd;
It is for his sake, this holiday we make,
An sooa let his health gooa rahnd.

Cutler, A. Morrow, 1875.

Shepherd Wheel by Peter Fairclough, 1992

These words form part of the lyrics to an unusual CD of modern jazz produced by the Fairclough Group in 1995. The words and music evoke the unique atmosphere of the once industrial valley, using many of the unusual trade terms once familiar to the local grinders. The wtaer wheel itself was frequently referred to as the dairy maid.

Little London Wheel, River Sheaf 1975, Peter Machan

In the rain, the rhythms of the water,
From the Mayfield flows the River Porter
Through the head goit, the dam, the sluice
The running water turns the Wheel.

The Wheel turns the drive-shaft in the hull.
The belt goes to the pulley through the bearstake.
Across the robin, lean on the blade
Against the stone face which turns away.

The 'Dairy Maid' will freeze up in the winter.
If you don't keep a dolly in your trow your stone gets hot.
The water cools the turning stone,
The grey stone whets the foaming blade.

The Cutler's Daughter by E. Darbyshire, 1885

I particularly like this poem because in it Darbyshire so cleverly uses his knowledge of the pocket knife trade to introduce so much of the craft's vocabulary into an altogether different context. 'Tommy's' refers to Tommy Youden, the proprietor of the Music Hall on Westbar.

>I'm a blade, rough handled, fluted and spangled,
>>My heart is entangled with love, true as steel,
>For a poor cutler's daughter, who lives in the quarter,
>>Where rough Sheffield grinders turn many wheel.
>She's made of such metal, wild hearts she can settle,
>>She's pretty well polished - she's everything nice;
>For when I first met her, and tried hard to get her,
>>I felt like a pocket knife screwed in a vice.

Buffing Electro-Plate, 1869.

>Industrious rather, she works with her father,
>>Pinning on scale tangs from morning to night;
>And charming Susannah, she sings to her hammer,
>>And needs no piano to keep her notes bright.

The grinders have made her as sharp as a razor,
    A witty young shaver, so careless and free;
She's a blade for a sportsman, a match for a foreman-
    In fact she's too good for a waster like me.

*Ida Thompson, Fork Buffing, Arundel Street, 1980,
Peter Machan.*

I'll make her my dear wife, then, like a penknife,
    I'll flourish my feathers whene'er duty calls;
And polish my manners, like charming Susannah's,
    And take her to Tommy's to dances and balls.
And should Fortune's chances e'er lop off the branches,
    Of our little business, though small it may be;
You cutlers shall never say you put together,
  Round tangs, or scale tangs, paired better than we.

The Grinder from 'The Village Patriot'
by Ebenezer Elliott 1815

Elliott brings us back to the bleak reality of the atrocious working conditions in which a grinder, daily inhaling the deadly cocktail of sandstone and steel particles which flew from the stone, would be lucky to live much beyond thirty.

> Where toils the mill by ancient woods embraced,
> Hark how the cold steel screams in hissing fire!
> There draws the grinder his laborious breath;
> There coughing at his deadly trade he bends.
> Born to die young, he fears nor man nor death;
> Scorning the future, what he earns he spends;
> Debauch and riot are his bosom friends.

Studies of grinders by H.P. Parker, 1840s.

Tally i o, the Grinder! — Traditional, 19th century.

Carved Brick Relief of a Grinder on Wall of 'The Jolly Buffer', Ecclesall Road. (Photo: Peter Machan)

1. The Sheffield grinder's a terrible blade,
   Tally i o, the grinder!
   He sets his little ones down to trade,
   Tally i o, the grinder!
   He turns his baby to grind in the hull
   Till his body is stunted, his eyes are dull,
   And his brains are dizzy and dazed in his skull,
   Tally i o, the grinder!

2. He shortens his life as he hastens his death,
   Tally i o, the grinder!
   Will drink steel dust in every breath;
   Tally i o, the grinder!
   Won't use the fan when he turns the wheel,
   Won't wash his hands ere he eats his meal,
   But dies as he lives, as hard as steel,
   Tally i o, the grinder!

3. At whose door lies the blacker blame?
   Tally i o, the grinder!
   Where rests the heavier weight of shame?
   Tally i o, the grinder!
   On the famine-price contractor's head,
   Or the workman's under taught and fed,
   Who grinds his own bones, and his child's for his bread?
   Tally i o, the grinder!

The Grinder's Hardships
Traditional, about 1805.

This song, which appears in the collection of works by Joseph Mather, has become one of the best known traditional Sheffield classics. It so clearly reiterates the daily hardships faced by the grinders that it really is difficult to understand how anyone could put up with such conditions. As well as the ever present danger from the dust this song also mentions the danger from being hit by a heavy piece of the grindstone if it should suddenly burst under him. This eventuality was not unknown.

A Sheffield Grinders 'Hull', 1862.

To be a Sheffield grinder it is no easy life,
There's more than you'd imagine to the grinding of a knife,
The oldest man amongst us is old at thirty two,
There's few who brave such hardships as we poor grinders do.

It happened in the year eighteen hundred and five
From May Day to Christmas the season was quite dry,
That all our oldest grinders such a time never knew,
For there's few who brave such hardships as we poor grinders do.

In summer we can't work until water does appear,
And if this does not happen the season is severe,
Then our fingers they are numbed by keen winter frost or snow,
There's few who brave such hardships as we poor grinders do.

When our country goes to war our mesters quickly cry,
'Orders countermanded' our goods we all lay by,
Your prices we must settle, and you'll be stinted too,
There's few who brave such hardships as we poor grinders do.

And every working day we are breathing dust and steel,
And a broken stone can give us that wound that will not heal,
There's many an honest grinder ground down by such a blow,
There's few who brave such hardships as we poor grinders do.

Grinder's Hull, City Centre, 1875, by A. Morrow. Notice the broken stone.

There's many a poor grinder whose family is large,
That, with all his best endeavours, cannot his debts discharge,
And when his children cry for bread, how pitiful to view,
There's few who brave such hardships as we poor grinders do.

So now I must conclude these few and humble lines
With 'success to every grinder as suffers in hard times'
I wish them better fortune, and all their family too,
For there's few who brave such hardships as we poor grinders do.

File-Cutters Lament
from Pawson and Brailsford's Guide, 1862.

Although we can imagine little more laborious work than to sit day in, day out, punching every tooth into every file by hand, as Mother so clearly demonstrates in 'The File Hewer's Lamentation' the file cutters fiercely resisted any attempt to mechanise the craft until late in the nineteenth century. This poem, if it deserves the name, was written in response to the news that a firm in Manchester had introduced a machine which may well have posed a threat to their livelihoods. The second poem on the same subject, although written at a similar date, takes a quite different view of the prosperity created by heavy machinery. For a hundred years most Sheffield folk were lulled to sleep by the reassuring reverberations of the heavy forging hammers, now silenced, in the steel works strung along the Don and Sheaf valleys.

Steam Hammer, Messrs. Sanderson Bros. and Co, Attercliffe, 1862.

It's the wonder of wonders, this mighty steam hammer,

What folks say it will do, it would make anyone stammer;

They say it will cut files as fast as three men and a lad,

But two out of three, it's a fact, they are bad.

They say it will strike 300 strokes in a minute

If this is a fact, there will be something serious in it;

The tooth that is on them looks fine to the eye,

But they're not worth a rush when fairly they're tried.

These Manchester cotton lords seem mighty keen

To take trade from old Sheffield with this cutting machine:

They've a secret to learn- they know it's a truth

The machine's naught like flesh and blood to raise up a tooth.

So unite well together, by good moral means,

Don't be intimidated by these infernal machines;

Let them boast as they will- and though the press clamour,

After all lads, there's nothing like wrist, chisel and hammer.

150 ton high-speed Forging Press by Davy Bros. 1908.

The Steam Hammer,
Dedicated to those living in its Vicinity   by John Hall, 1874

6,000 ton Forging Press, John Brown's, 1911.

Thud! Thud! Thud!
   Cough! Cough! Cough!
Like a giant with asthma,
   And a voice both hoarse and rough;
You hear the big steam hammer,
   Pounding at his mill;
Steady and slow, with measured blow,
   And a steel and iron will.

Thud! Thud! Thud!
   When eyes are heavy for sleep;
And cough! Cough! Cough!
   When the day begins to peep.
Is it he fabled Vulcan,
   With his one-eyed Cyclops band,
Forging the thunderbolts of Jove
   With never wearied hand?

Would you view the giant-
    Monster though he be-
Crushing ponderous ingots,
    Terrible to see?
Yet he can be gentle,
    Tractable and mild,
And will crack a nut, or break an egg,
    As softly as a child.

See his huge arm raising
    At the prompter's call!
Yet a touch will turn it
    And moderate the fall.
Such is all true greatness-
    In the power of might,
Ready to do a little thing
    If only it be right.

Thud! Thud! Thud!
    See what it has wrought!
Fortune upon fortune,
    Hammered out of nought;
Almshouses and churches,-
    Palaces and parks,
And everywhere prosperity
    The product of its sparks!

Cough! Cough! Cough!
    Through the midnight deep,
It is earning thousands
    While the owners sleep;
It is toiling for a nation
    And all the world beside;
For railways, ships and arsenals,
    O'er lands and oceans wide!

Let it thud and thunder-
    Let it cough and groan-
Though our rest be broken
    We will not bemoan,
But honour the steam giant-
    The Vulcan of our time;
No myth of old mythology,
    But a working power sublime!

John Brown & Co. and the Sheffield Armour Plates
by Richard Nesbitt Ryan, 1861.

Both the subject and the author of this poem are fascinating. Ryan was one of the most colourful characters of nineteenth century Sheffield. He was a showman as well as a prolific versifier. He was the first lessee of the Royal Amphitheatre, a remarkable construction at the end of Blonk Street which included a huge circus ring. A playbill for May 1838 advertised *Paul Pry*, performed on horseback by Mr. Ryan, who will play six different characters! On the night of the Great Sheffield Flood in 1864 he was lodging at a house on Wicker Lane which was flooded and most of his writings were destroyed. The compensation commissioners awarded him £100, a third of the sum that he claimed for the loss of his manuscripts.

It was in 1860 that John Brown of the great Atlas steel works constructed a huge rolling mill capable of producing the 5-ton armour plate four and a half inches thick which protected the 'Warrior', the first of the ironclad battleships. A piece of this plate can be seen at Kelham Island Museum.

> John Brown & Co. are famous men,
>   Beloved by all the town.
> Their like shall ne'er be seen again,
>   We honour their renown.
> Their Armour Plates have stood the test
>   The Armstrong guns have hurled;
> It is confessed they are the best
>   Of any in the world.
>
>   Hey! John Brown & Co.!
>   O! John Brown & Co.!
>   Old and young
>   Their praise have sung
>   John Brown & Co.!

All praise be to John Brown & Co.
   Who work our ships to shield
'Gainst shot from any foreign foe,
   Who ne'er can make us yield.
To guard our rights we're ever brave,
   Our might we wish to shew
Britannia ever rules the wave
   God bless John Brown & Co.!

      Hey! John Brown & Co.!
      O! John Brown & Co.!
      Old and young
      Their praise have sung
      John Brown & Co.!

Rolling a 20-ton armour plate, John Brown's, 1861

The 'Warrior' shall uphold its name
    Clothed in its coat of mail.
Its deeds enhancing England's fame
    We know no word called 'fail.'
Our ships impregnable shall be
    That plough the mighty main,
The monarchs of the rolling sea
    That ever will remain.

        Hey! John Brown & Co.!
        O! John Brown & Co.!
        Old and young
        Their praise have sung
        John Brown & Co.!

They merits all the great renown
    Upon them now awaits;
A credit to old Sheffield town
    Are John Brown's Armour Plates.
Though cannon balls fall thick as rain
    'Tis victory we mean;
Our enemies, then strive in vain
    God bless our noble Queen!

        Hey! John Brown & Co.!
        O! John Brown & Co.!
        Old and young
        Their praise have sung
        John Brown & Co.!

The Whittlesmith's Lamentation   by Joseph Senior, 1882

If anyone was qualified to write with such bitterness about his life in the blade-forging trade it was surely Joseph Senior. Writing late in life, as his eyesight was fading, the 'Smithy Bard' leaves us with no feelings of the romance of a working life, simply utter weariness. Typically of the Sheffield trades, he was, together with his three brothers, part of the third generation of his family to work as blade-forgers at 'The Old Number 6 Norfolk Street' the world famous works of Joseph Rodgers and Sons. His own sons were to follow.

Forger, Garden Street, 1975.

Be silent my anvil and hammer,
Whilst Somnus bequeaths me a boon;
For you've thump'd my eardrums with your clamour,
'Till my brain 'gins to waltz to your tune.

A wearier bard never sang you,
Since Vulcan went 'prentice I'll wage;
Ten thousand long days I have rang you,
And all for untimely old age.

I once thought your music was bracing,
But now 'tis portentous of gloom
-Slow, limping, and dull, like the pacing
Of weary bones seeking a tomb.

The Norton Scythesmith's Song   Anon* 1814.

Written on the event of group of Norton scythesmiths being sentenced to a spell in Derby Jail (Norton Village was then in Derbyshire) for 'combining' or coming together to ask for an increase in wages in May, 1814, trade union activity being illegal.

Norton Church and the Chantrey Memorial

At the Bowling Green the meeting was held,
We Journeyman scythesmiths there did attend;
We drew up the statement as all had agreed
And sent to our masters, but did not succeed.

We were summoned the magistrate's court to attend;
Justice Jebb and Sir William nine of us did send
(because we'd no money nor friend to give bail)
For a fortnight free lodging in Derby jail.

And when we got there some drinking, some smoking,
While others looked sad,
We thought it was Bedlam
and all going mad.

Hard boards and Long Straw we had for our Beds,
We pulled off our Breeches to put under our Heads,
We pulled off our Coats for both Blanket and Sheet,
We pulled off our Waistcoats to wrap our cold feet.

* Quoted in 'Chantreyland' by Harold Armitage, .

Cutler's Poetry,

Traditionally inscribed on the blades of folding knives during the 17th century, couplets like these were well enough known for Shakespeare to refer to them in The Merchant of Venice as follows-

Portia.   A quarrel, ho, already? What's the matter?

Gratiano.   About a hoop of gold, a paltry ring
                    That she did give me: whose posy was,
                    For all the world like cutler's poetry,
                    Upon a knife, '*Love me, and leave me not*'

Nerissa.   What! Talk you of the posy or the value?
                    You swore to me, when I did give it you,
                    That you would wear it till your hour of death.

                                                 Act V Scene 1

Sheffield made, both haft and blade,
London for you life, show me such a knife.

       Sharpen me well and keep me clean,
           And I'll cut my way through fat and lean.

I'm a Sheffield blade 'tis true
Pray what sort of blade are you?

         To carve your meate is my intent,
           Use me, but let me not be lent.

I'll wait upon you at the table,
And doe what service I am able.

                 Let mee not long
                 Where cooks are throng.

The Toll-Bar Keeper by John Hall, 1874.

The site of the subject of this poem, the Stoney Ridge Toll Bar, is commemorated by a stone beside the road at the summit of the moor just before reaching Fox House. It's a wild and windy spot and hardly surprising that, once the bar was abolished in 1884, and Samuel Barton the keeper to whom the poem refers was no longer required to exact the tolls from passing travellers, the cottage was allowed to fall into ruin.

High on the Longshawe Moors,
  High upon Peak's grey mountains,
Where the Burbage babbles and brawls,
  In a hundred crystal fountains;

Here an old toll-bar stands,
  On a ridge that is rugged and stoney;
Bare on the moorland heath,
  The haunt of the grouse and coney.

And here, too, the old toll-keeper
  Stands at his post of duty,
Taxing the traveller's purse,
  Regardless of wealth or beauty.

He keeps a few pigs and a cow,
  That feed on the wayside herbage;
And cobbles the boots of his neighbours,
  From Grindleford up to Burbage.

Ever a smile has he,
  And ever a friendly greeting,
Whatever the weather may be,
  Snowing, raining or sleeting.

He cares not for thunder or lightning,
  Hurricane or tornado,
And laughs at the roaring wind
  As though it were all bravado.

When dreary winter comes
  And the snow lies thick around him,
He chuckles and mends the fire,
  And thinks how well off 't has found him.

And when glad summer returns,
  And the bloom is on the heather,
When the Cuckoo and Ring-ouzel
  Perch on the wall together,

You'll see him in his garden,
  Hoeing, digging or weeding,
Or out upon the roadside
  His various poultry feeding,

And when the sun goes down
  O'er the rocks of Higgin, westward,
He will smoke his pipe with the keepers
  Returning home and restward.

Death and Disaster

From The Cholera Mount

By James Montgomery, 1832

With many apologies, I include only one of the hundreds of verses composed by one of Sheffield's most famous poets and hymnwriters, James Montgomery, but I think that it will be only too clear why his verse is so out of fashion today! The sentiments expressed are those familiar from so much of nineteenth century poetry, most forcibly reiterated in the last line, in case anyone were in any doubt, but to the population of a filthy, insanitary town, ravaged by disease and absorbed by the idea of an early death, such sentiments were most pertinent. The burial place, somewhat surprisingly compared here to Siberia, was in fact on the hillside above Shrewsbury Road and the fine memorial, the *'statelier honours'* for which Montgomery was instrumental in raising the finance to build, rises above the present Midland Station. The cholera outbreak, the *'blue pest'*, killed 402 people during the summer of 1832 but Montgomery was clearly as ill-informed as most people of his time about its cause. We now know that it was contracted, not through an air-borne infection, but through ingesting water contaminated with the cholera bacteria. The poem has the following cumbersome sub-title *'Lines on the burying place of the disease in 1832, and while great terror of infection from it was experienced throughout the kingdom, sanctioned by legislative authority requiring the separate interment of its unfortunate victims.'*

In death divided from their dearest kin,
This is 'a field to bury strangers in;'
Fragments, from families untimely reft,
Like spoils in flight or limbs in battle left,
Lie here;- a sad community, whose homes
Might feel, methinks a pang to quicken stones;
While from beneath my feet they seem to cry,
'Oh! Is it nought to you, ye who pass by!
When from its earthly house the spirit fled,
Our dust may not be 'free among the dead?'
Ah! Why were to this Siberia sent,
Doom'd in the grave itself to banishment?'

Shuddering humanity asks, 'Who are these?
And what their crime?' ***They fell by one disease!***
By the blue pest, whose gripe no art can shun,
No force unwrench, out-singled one by one;
When, like a monstrous birth, the womb of fate
Bore a new death of unrecorded date,
And doubtful name. Far east the fiend began
Its course; thence round the world pursued the sun,
The ghosts of millions following at its back,
Whose desecrated graves betray'd their track.
On Albion's shores unseen the invader slept;
Secret and swift through the field and city swept;
At noon, at midnight, seized the weak, the strong,
Asleep, awake, alone, amid the throng:
Kill'd like a murderer; fix'd its icy hold,
And wrung out life with agony of cold;
Nor stay'd its vengeance where it crush'd its prey,
But set a mark, like Cain's, upon their clay,
And this tremendous seal impress'd on all,-
'Bury me out of sight and out of call.'

With statelier honours still, in time's slow round,
Shall this sepulchral eminence be crown'd,
Where generations long to come shall hail
The growth of centuries waving in a gale,
A forest landmark on the mountain's head,
Standing betwixt the living and the dead,
Nor, while your language lasts, shall traveller cease,
To say, at sight of your memorial, *'Peace!'*
Your voice of silence answering from the soul,
'Whoe'er thou art, prepare to meet thy God!'

*James Montgomery's Memorial Statue in its original position in the General Cemetery.
It now stands beside the Cathedral.*

The Great Sheffield Flood
March 11th, 1864

The appalling events of the night of March 11th 1864, when the Dale Dike reservoir burst its banks releasing a wall of water to sweep down the Loxley Valley causing immense destruction and the death of almost two hundred and fifty people was poetically the most widely recorded event in Sheffield's history. In the days following the disaster self-styled poets hawked their penny sheets of doggerel verse to the crowds of sightseers who flocked to the site. Most of their offerings rival McGonagall in their banality.

This first poem, however, was printed in Alfred Gatty's edition of Hunter's Hallamshire, of 1869. He describes it as being written by a friend.

A Hopeless Case,   by Patrick Scott 1864

    T'was the dead of night, when on Sheffield town
      And her sleeping sons and daughters,
    With its voice of a thunderous hiss came down
      The avalanche of waters.

    There was silence in each doomed abode,
      No light showed the fate before them;
    When the lake burst forth from its bounds, and flowed
      In a measureless cataract o'er them.

    Mother and maiden, old men and young,
      Were mixed in one quick, deep burying;
    Like wild flowers wrenched from its banks, and flung
      In the path of a torrent hurrying.

    The strong man struggled not then-no scream
      From the lips of the infant sounded-
    Hope raised not her head o'er the whelming stream
      Where darkness and death abounded.

    The building that was based on a rock,
      The tree that had lived through ages,
    Were swept from the earth by that ocean shock,
      Like a blot we wipe from our pages.

    No time for prayer in that sudden flood,
      No space for the soul's repentance,
    As if the destroying angel stood,
      And struck ere he spoke their sentence.

How many in England, wrapped in sleep,
  Slept on in unchanged position,
Through the hours wherein the remorseless deep
  Went forth on its terrible mission!

Then mercy-oh! Mercy for those who died
  In that night of blinding terrors;
When the breath was choked, ere the lips had cried,
  "Oh Father, forgive our errors!"

The Ruins of Rowel Bridge Grinding Wheels.

Gravestones of the Victims of the Sheffield Flood * 1864.

SUDDEN THE GUSH 'TWAS THUS SHE FELL,
NOT EVEN TIME TO BID HER FRIENDS
FAREWELL.

Sarah Mount, aged 40,
swept out of her
shop at Malin Bridge.

*Armitage Family Gravestone,
Loxley Chapel.*

LIKE CROWNED FOREST TREES WE STAND,
AND SOME ARE MARK'D TO FALL,
THE AXE WILL SMITE AT GOD'S COMMAND,
AND SOON SHALL SMITE US ALL.

Charles Price, 50, Elizabeth, 50, Edward, 24,
Sarah (his wife) John (their son) 1 year 8 months
and an unnamed infant, also from Malin Bridge.

THE ROSE IN ITS BRIGHTEST BLOOM,
THE SUN'S BRIGHTEST GLORIES DECLINE;
SO EARLY CAME I TO THE TOMB,
REPENT LEST THE CASE SHOULD BE THINE.
THE BUSY TRIBES OF FLESH AND BLOOD,
WITH ALL THEIR CARES AND FEARS;
ARE CARRIED ONWARD BY THE FLOOD,
AND LOST FOLLOWING YEARS.

Elizabeth Crownshaw aged 17.

* The first four gravestones are to be found in the overgrown graveyard of Loxley Reform Chapel and the Trickett's is in Bradfield churchyard.

THE EVILS THAT BEST OUR PATH,
WHO CAN PREVENT OR CURE;
WE STAND UPON THE BRINK OF DEATH,
WHEN MOST WE SEEM SECURE;
IF WE TODAY SWEET PEACE POSSESS,
IT SOON MAY BE WITHDRAWN;
SOME CHANGE MAY PLUNGE US IN DISTRESS,
BEFORE TOMORROW'S MORN.

The Armitage Family of the Malin Bridge Inn.

The Trickett's Gravestone

AMID THE SOLEMN MIDNIGHT HOUR
BORNE BY THE FLOOD WITH MIGHTY POWER
THEY SANK BENEATH A WATERY GRAVE,
INTO HIS ARMS WHO'S STRONG TO SAVE.

The Trickett Family,
all eleven of whom died
when the flood swept away their
farmhouse at Malin Bridge.

Lines on the Great Flood, which occurred at Sheffield, through the bursting of the Bradfield Dam, twixt the hours of 12 and 1 o'clock, on the morning of Saturday, March 12th 1864.

by J.B. Geoghegan

The stars hung high o'er Loxley Vale, the cattle sought the shed,
The tiny stream danc'd gaily on, along its pebbly bed,
The sheep were gather'd in the fold, the bird had found its nest,
And babes were nustled peacefully, beside the mother's breast;
The strong man worn out with his toil, and children with their play,
Had sought alike the sleep that gives new strength to meet the day,
And many a lov'd and loving form, had clos'd the weary eye,
In slumbers, never more to wake, or but to wake and die!

The cheerful lisp, the merry laugh, the cold or kindly word
Was whisper'd but in silent dreams, and scarce a breath was heard,
Save but the wind, which at the close of day had been a breeze,
That now had sprung into a gale, and whistled thro' the trees;
But hark, that strange tumultuous sound!- whence comes that deaf'ning roar?
Like some stupendous avalanche dash'd on a storm toss'd shore;
The pent up floods in Bradfield Dam have burst the basin huge,
And now come thundering down the steep in one mad wild deluge.

And soon the streams became as brooks, the brooks as rivers wide,
And all the valley one vast sea, lash'd up by angry tide.
And furiously the bursting wave rushed through the ravine drear,
Destroying all, and everything that crossed its dread career;
The sturdy oak, the towering elm, were snapp'd in twain like reeds,
And ponderous stones borne high along, as ripples bear the weeds;

And bridges crumbl'd 'neath the rush, the earth was torn and rent,
And massive blocks and iron beams like twigs were writh'd and bent.
The farm, the homestead and the forge, the wheelhouse and the mill,
And whatsoever man had made, of science and of skill,
The workman's hut, the rich man's store, the wealth and toil of years,
Were lost! And where a village stood a wilderness appears.

And high above the water's roar was heard the voice of prayer;
Man's agonising cry for help, his wail of wild despair.
For mid the wash of barn and field, the roots and trees uptorn,
Swift on the billows surging breast, both man and beast were borne;
The aged matron, and the maid, the husband and the wife,
The grandsire and the infant babe, new struggling into life,
Alike were with the torrent swept, that from the dam tore down
In one fierce foaming cateract, o'erwhelming half the town!

At length the day's stars rays shone out, the night clouds drifted by,
The sun rose calmly in the east and tinged with gold the sky;
But what a sight his light reveal'd, - what desolation dire,
Enough t'appal the stoutest heart and set the brain on fire.
Far, far as e'er the eye could reach, sad evidence was seen,
How strong and mighty was the flood, how fierce its rage had been,
So wide-spread was the havoc made, so vasty was the blight,
Imagination cannot paint the ruin wrought that night!

From Bradfield hills to Bradfield dale, Damflask and Malin Bridge,
And all along the green-bank side, the gorge and o'er the ridge,
From Loxley on to Owlerton, across and o'er Neepsend;
And down the valley of the Don, I every turn and bend,
From Hillsbro' on to Harvest Lane, and all the lowlands round,
Along the Wicker and its ways, wher'ere a path was found,
The huge uprorious sea had work'd its devastating track,
Engulphing all within its reach in universal wrack.-

Uprooted trees, logs, bales and beams, great heaps of brick and stone
And mighty engines, ripp'd and crack'd, like toys about were thrown,
A thousand beings homeless made, upon the damp ground stood,
Pale, shivering in the cold March wind, knee deep in slime and mud,
And o'er the waste of sludge and mire, stern men in bands were spread,

Close eying every chink and nook,- the searchers for the dead!
And children for their fathers wept, and fathers for their sons,
And mothers, scarcely mothers made, wept for their little ones.
The widow mourn'd the husband lost, the husband moun'd the wife,
And everywhere was heard a wail for loss of human life!
Thus perish'd nigh three hundred souls beneath the boiling wave,
For tho' men heard their cries for help, they had no power to save.

O man! How vain thy boasted skill, how feeble is thy power,
To Him, who can the work of years, destroy in one short hour,
To thy ambition, Sheffield lays this elemental strife,
This wide expanse of misery, and fearful loss of life!
But while a throb beats in the heart, or mem'ry holds her throne,
God grant the like calamity may ne'er again be known.

The Ruins of Malin Bridge.

Sheffield Blitz
by A.F.S., Dedicated to t'Wife. 1941.*

Memories of the night of December 12th 1940 are here evoked in this narrative poem by a member of the Auxiliary Fire Service. It was on this night that Sheffield suffered its heaviest bombing. The city centre was well ablaze at midnight, the height of the nine hour ordeal. High Street and the Moor were flattened and it was possible to read a newspaper at Broomhill by the light of the city burning. The casualties of both service personnel and civilians reached the hundreds, but the vital steel works, stretched along the Don Valley, lay under a protective shroud of mist, and apparently escaped major damage. I suspect that the writer of this poem, to judge by his plea in the last verse, would have been somewhat disappointed by the post war rebuilding programme.

An early moon was near its height-
It touched the frosty roofs with light;
A swirling mist rose near the Don-
We hoped t'would thicken later on:
And when the siren's mournful scream
Came echoing like some ghostly theme,
We sniffed the mist and scanned the sky,
And thought 'Maybe they'll pass us by!'

But no! At last our turn had come!
The skies re-echoed with the hum
Of bombing planes, their task so clear
To wreck our town and teach us fear.
A grim diapason of sound;
A stealthy shudder of the ground;
An evil glow, as if the flame
Which pierced the darkness, felt some shame.

* Printed in 'All Clear' the monthly magazine of the ARP wardens, may 1941

Now A.F.S. quit you like men
T'will never be the same again.
This winter night the stars look down
On yet another martyred town.
The fire calls come, the pumps speed forth;

We've got to dare the gates of wrath:
London and Coventry, we know
Were brave. God grant we may be so!

Beside the causeway edge, a snake
Of darkling canvas lies
And as we watch, it seems to wake,
Swelling, before our eyes.
And water in a gleaming jet
Leaps to attack the flame;
The fireman with his body set
Stands firm, determined, game.

And now is heard a note more shrill
As hissing founts of steam
Rise from the burning embers, till
The glow fades to a gleam.
Far up the ladders in the night
A swaying figure looms,
His axe the symbol of the fight-
'Tis thus that courage blooms.

"Light in, light in*, you sons of sin,
let's have more ruddy hose;

we'll have to get much further in
before the main block goes".
The blasted pump is running hot-
Our hands are bruised and cold,
Still, it's the only one we've got,
Let's hope that it will hold!

The ambulances come and go
Despite the hellish rain,
And one receives a mortal blow-
It will not serve again.
St. John Brigade again have made
The eternal sacrifice,
Yet still they come on, unafraid,
Willing to pay the price.

What is that curious note long drawn?
Why are the guns so still?
Yet there remain four hours till dawn

* A fire brigade term meaning to pull out more hose

Comes creeping o'er the hill.
The moon is pale in the furnace glow-
The bombers all have gone......
Though many the sunrise ne'er may know
We, who are left, fight on.

And now the icy wraith of fear
Forms like some evil gnome.
How have they fared who we hold dear-
What are things like at home?
A spate of rumours fan our doubt
Our brain's on fire; though calm without
We cannot rest in any place
Until we meet them face to face.

I passed by Sheffield in the morn
From Greenland Road to Arbourthorne;
I saw the distant fires ablaze
And mused how strange are fortune's ways,
Hundreds of folk, as good as I,
Beneath the tangled wreckage lie.
Lord, grant to us who still remain
Vision to build our town again!

To the People of Sheffield
by S.May, December 1940*.

Here's to the lads of the A.R.P.
And the lads of the A.F.S.;
And here's to the lasses! We all agree
That they served their city, I guess.
Here's to the stalwart lads in blue,
For they played their part right well:
Here's to the Ambulance units, too,
Who worked through a blinding hell!

Here's to the Doctors and Nurses too.
The call on their skill was immense:
And here's to each service that toiled the night through.
Each member of Civil Defence!
Here's to the women and kids so brave,
Whose part was to 'sit it through';
And here's to the homeless, with nothing to save
But their spirit, still loyal and true!

Here's to you all, who will battle again,
If called to re-enter the fray,
…Our loved ones were slain, but they died not in vain;
In dying, they pointed the way!
And here's to the City of Steel so proud
(As its steel, may it ever be true!);
O, people of Sheffield, unbent and unbowed;
Stout hearts - *we* are proud of YOU!

*From 'All Clear' The Magazine of the Sheffield ARP Wardens, No.7, December 1940.

Remembering the Mi Amigo.
by Susan, Lisa and Margaret Anderson. 2002

I copied this piece from a typed sheet attached to the memorial to the American airmen who were killed when their flying fortress crashed in Endcliffe Park. The attendant myth which has grown up around this story, that the pilot sacrificed their lives to save children playing on the field is unfortunately not borne out by the contemporary accounts.

> A large crowd gathered on the hillside
> Bathed in the morning sunlight of early spring,
> As we remembered the brave crew of Mi Amigo,
> And heard the plaintive songs of birds on the wing.

> It was many years since those men lost their lives
> And smoke and flames billowed from the stricken plane,
> We owed such a debt to those gallant young men,
> Who were destined never to return home again.

> As I stood amongst others in respectful silence
> I reflected on the workings of fate and its mysterious way,
> I glanced across at my home that could have been my tomb,
> And thought of those generations who may not have been
>   here today.

> It was a long time ago that our lives were spared,
> When the doomed plane crashed in the park,
> But for many it seems like only yesterday
> That world war two was fought in times grim and hard.

In stark contrast the woods are now calm and peaceful,
But we can never forget the price that those airmen paid,
As in this little quiet and green corner of England
Our wreaths of remembrance are carefully laid.

As we now honour those airmen who passed away
In that tragic event on the leafy wooded slope,
We know that they did not perish in vain without purpose,
For they left behind memories of courage and hope.

Painting by Elizabeth Mottram of Mi Amigo over Endcliffe Park

They sacrificed their tomorrows for our future,
As their plane fell to ground on the bleak hillside,
But as their spirits soured free to heaven
Their names were to be evermore carved with pride.

So this morning we pay our respects to the fallen,
As shots from a 21-gun salute rents the chill air,
We listen to the poignant sounds of the lone piper
And the Last Post in memory of those no longer there.

Gravestone of William Hobson
who died in 1815

BENEATH THIS STONE A GRINDER LIES,
A SUDDEN DEATH ATH CLOSED HIS EYES;
HE LOST HIS LIFE BY THE BREAKING OF A STONE,
WE HOPE HIS SOUL TO HEAVEN HAS GONE,

Gravestone to Favourite Horse, Stafford Lane, Norfolk Park.

I have only recently discovered this remarkable monument. It stands against a wall at the gin stables, on Stafford Lane, the place where the horses which worked at the Duke of Norfolk's collieries in the Park, were stabled. The date has unfortunately worn away but the style suggests that it dates from the mid nineteenth century. Who was the horse? Was he called 'Steady'? For what cause did he die? Is he actually buried here or did he die bravely in battle as the inscription suggests? There is an intriguing story behind this but, like so much of Sheffield's fascinating history, it has been sadly forgotten.

THE BRAVE HORSES YIELD,
THE PROUD STEADY'S GONE;
HE FELL IN THE CAUSE,
WHERE OFT HE LED ON.

LIKE A WARRIOR STRUCK DOWN,
WHERE BRITAINS SHOUT BRAVE,
THIS, THE PLACE OF HIS TRIUMPHS,
THE SPOT OF HIS GRAVE.

W. Turner

THIS STONE IS ERECTED HERE IN
MEMORY OF MY FAVOURITE HORSE.

W. Turner

Epitaph to Mark Tyzack of Four lane Ends, blacksmith, from his gravestone in Norton Churchyard, dated 1795.

MY SCYTHE AND HAMMER LIES RECLIN'D
MY BELLOWS TOO HAS LOST THEIR WINDE
MY IRON IS SPENT MY STEEL IS GONE
MY SCYTHES ARE SET MY WORK IS DONE
MY FIRES EXTINCT MY FORGE DECAY'D
MY BODY IN THE DUST IS LAID.

Gravestone in Handsworth Churchyard

LIKE NIMROD I DID RANGE THE FIELD
FOR GAME WITH DOG AND GUN;
TILL GOD DID PLEASE TO MAKE ME YIELD
IN FATAL RIVER DUN.
A WARNING TAKE MY COMRADES ALL
OF DRINKING TO EXCESS;
BE READY WHEN THE LORD DOTH CALL
THAT HE MAY YE ALL BLESS.

John Knott, Scissor-Grinder, Sheffield *

HERE LIES A MAN THAT WAS KNOTT BORN,
HIS FATHER WAS KNOTT BEFORE HIM;
HE LIVED KNOTT, AND DID KNOTT DIE,
YET UNDERNEATH THIS STONE, KNOTT BEGOT
AND HERE HE LIES AND YET WAS KNOTT.

* Collected in 'A Yorkshire Anthology' by J. Horsfall Turner, pub. Bradford, 1901. The location of this singularly witty epitaph is unfortunately not recorded. Presumably it was in the old graveyard of the Parish Church.

Sheffield Cemetery   by Leapidge Smith, 1854.*

The General Cemetery opened in 1836 on carefully landscaped grounds on the north facing side of the Porter Valley. It catered for the new middle class residents of Nether Edge and Sharrow and many of the town's illustrious citizens lie buried there. It was formerly far more extensive than we see it today, since, in a deplorable act of vandalism, thousands of gravestones were bulldozed and buried in 1978. The conservation efforts of the Friends of the General Cemetery are to be congratulated.

The General Cemetery by Hofland, 1837.

> The bloody fields of Waterloo,
> Numbered its victims less than you,**
> Behold, with reverence and with fear
> How many dead lie waiting here
>   All mingle Ashes, dust to dust!

---

*   Woodland Shadows' Pub. London, 1854.
** At this date there were 4550 interments in the General Cemetery compared to the 2432 killed at Waterloo.

The Suckling, and the hoary head;
The Mean, and he to honours bred,
    All mingle ashes, dust to dust!
The Scholar, the unlearned hind;
The Churlish, and the very kind;
    All mingle ashes, dust to dust!

The Temperate, and the Dissolute,
The Just Man, and the Knave so cute
    All mingle ashes, dust to dust!
The Miser, and the Liberal hand;
Peasant, and Magnate of the land
    All mingle ashes, dust to dust!

The Wrathful, and the meek in soul,
The Dives, who in wealth did roll;
    All mingle ashes, dust to dust!
The Christian, full of faith and love;
The man no fear, no love could move
    All mingle ashes, dust to dust!

These shall all on judgement Day
Rise up from their so mingled clay,
The dead in Christ to rise the first
To rise from this so mingled dust!

No line divides the Saints of God,***
Although they varied paths have trod,
In unison join the choir above,
In hymns of joy and songs of love.

***Referring to the wall which divided the dissenters' graves from the Anglicans'.

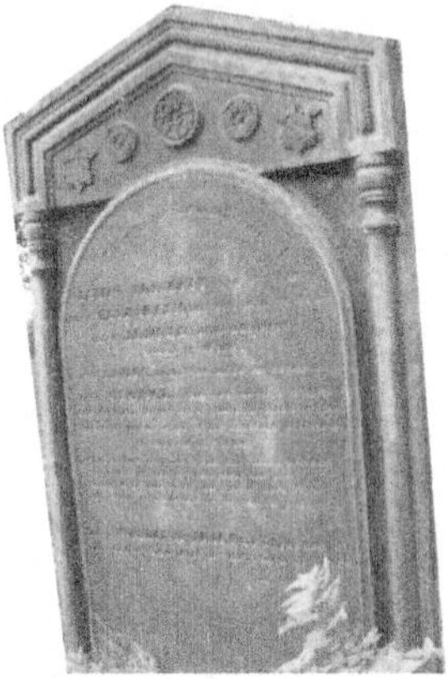

Fun and Frolics, Life and Love

Advertising Ditty
Anonymous, 19th Century

The Rose and Crown
In Sheffield town,
The landlord's named George Hartley,
He brews good ale,
It is not stale,
Where it is I'll tell you shortly.

It's in Waingate,
Which is not straight,
And leads into the Wicker,
Call as you pass, And take a glass,
'Twill make you travel quicker!

Little Sheffield Feast
From the Shevvild Chap's Song Book

A few months since on frolic bent,
On a journey to Little Sheffield Feast I went,
And being as all of us know quite gren'
I was mortally pleased with the sights I'd seen;
There was Betty and Jenny and Factory Nan,
And twenty more girls, and they each had a man,
And Sally and Sukey, and Bandy-legged Jack,
And the chap that sold pies with the can on his back.
There were donkeys and dog carts, and lots of fine folks,
With their jaws all a cracking their nuts and their jokes,
As hungry as hunters from biggest to least,
All right for a blow out at Little Sheffield Feast.

All the Fun of Sheffield Fair, 1905.

Yorkshire Ways   by C A Renshaw, 1922.*

How well Miss Renshaw captures the spirit of the age when, during the 1920s the battle to secure the right to roam over the moors above Sheffield's smoky suburbs was at its fiercest. It was during this time that access to the Longshaw estate of moorland and wooded gorge, which is so affectionately evoked here, was secured. This country, stretching into North Derbyshire, has long been considered to be Sheffield's 'green lung', the city's proudest joy and treasure!

April laughs in England, and the dewlit grass is shining,
Shaken into ecstasy by the little winds that blow.
Wonders of the open road are here for your divining,
-No one knows the joy of it as Yorkshire people know,
    Tramping in the early hours,
    Tramping through the dew-lit flowers
Just to watch the sunrise from the heights of Ringinglow!

Eager little hedges with hazel tassels swinging,
Trembling little celendines in every wooded nook,
Sweeps of windy heather where the bracken green is springing,
Beauty with its olden glamour everywhere you look!
    These things are for Yorkshire men,
    Loving field and moor and glen,
Lured from Sheffield's clamour by the song of Burbage Brook.

Out on open moorland you can hear the curlew screaming,
Screaming shrill defiance in a land where he is lord.
Stubborn Yorkshire fighters hear a pibroch through their dreaming,
Vision wind-tossed banners and the splendour of a sword,
    Knowing life a venture is
    Down through all the centuries,
Hearing screaming pibrochs** on the way the Grindleford!

---

*From 'Up From the Hills,' 1922, included in 'Yorkshire in Prose and Verse, an Anthology' by G.F. Wilson, Elkin, Mathews and Marrot Ltd, London, 1929.
***Pibroch*-The haunting music of the highland pipes.

Careless twisted roadways, and a hint of coming daisies,
Bilberry and cranberry on every rocky ledge,
Little bubbling waters where a ceaseless song of praise is,
Whispers in the rowans, and a whistling in the sedge.
      Yorkshire climbers never tire,
      Reaching to their heart's desire,
Climbing, to the shouting winds on rugged Curbar Edge.

Hill and stream and heathered moor; new woodlands green and golden:
Secret glades of mystery where rugged oaks have stood,
Swept by years of wind-and rainstorms, gnarled and grim and olden;
Yorkshire men have seen the in the Deeps of Padley Wood.
      And their hearts have dreamed again
      Truant bands of green-clad men
Threading ancient forests to the horn of Robin Hood.

Oh! The fragrant hawthorn hedge a cross a haunted gloaming,
Fields aglow with buttercups and white with daisy-foam!
Yorkshire hearts are gypsy-hearts, but ever they'll be homing,
Dreaming daisied meadow-lands wherever they may roam.
After many heart-break years
They will come again with tears.
    ....Little winding Yorkshire ways will call the dreamers home!

The Sheffield Cutler's Song
Traditional, 18th Century

This extract from 'The Cutler's Song', quoted by Abel Bywater *in The Sheffield Dialect* of 1839 and by Robert Leader in *Sheffield in the Eighteenth Century,* 1901, refers back to the roarings and rantings of the gallery audiences in the new playhouses such as the Assembly Rooms on Norfolk Street and the Theatre Royal as well as the older establishments like the Angel Inn, from which Angel Street gets its name, in the early years of the nineteenth century. Assaults and intimidation of the sort mentioned in the song were all too common, especially during the period of 1816 to 1821 when the fearsome tailor 'Jacky Blacker', who led marauding bands of bread rioters round the town during the day armed with a pike and a pistol, took to the theatre, styling himself 'King of the Gallery'.

The 'flat-backs' were cheap knives produced mainly by rough out-of-town cutlers in places like Wadsley and Heeley. 'Yellow bellies' was a term used to describe the grinders, derived from the fact that after a day's work they would be covered with the yellow dust from their sandstones and 'nickerpickers' were filecutters. This is one of the songs made famous by its being used in 'The Stirrings in Sheffield on Saturday Night' by Allan Cullen.

Cum all yo cuttlin heroes, where'ersome'er yo be,
All yo wot works on flat-backs, cum lissen unto me;
    A baskit for a shillin,
    To mak em we are willin,
Or swap em for red herrins, ahr bellies tube fillin,
Or swap em for red herrins, ahr bellies tube fillin.

A baskit full o' flat-backs o'm shure we'l mak, or mooar,
To ger reit into't gallera, whear we can rant an roar,
    Thro' flat-backs, stooans and sticks;
    Red herrins, booans and bricks;
If they dooant play Nanca's Fanca, or onna tune we fix,
We'l do the best at e'er we can to braik sum oer ther necks.

*Ernest Mills, Pocket Knife Cutler, 1985,
Peter Machan.*

T' yoller bellies an't nickerpeckers are wi us all combined,
An' when we get I' t' gallera, my lads, all in a mind,
    An then we stamp away,
    An mak Joe Taylor play,
'Nottingham Races' quickly, withaht ony mooar delay,
Or else we'll break his fiddlestick all in a mind, huzza!

The Jolly Grinder

Broadsheet Ballad published by Joseph Ford about 1840.

There was a jolly Grinder once,
Liv'd by the River Don;
He work'd and sang from morn till night,
And sometimes he'd work none!
But still the burden of this song,
As ever used to be-
'Tis never worthwhile to work too long,
For it doesn't agree with me.

He seldom on a Monday work'd,
Except near Christmas Day;
It was not the labour that he'd shun'
For it was easier far than play;
But still the burden of this song
For ever used to be-
"Tis never worth while to work too long,
For it doesn't agree with me!'

Grinder Toby Jug by John Sinclair's, modelled on Rowland Swinden.

A pale teetotaller chanced to meet
Our grinder one fine day,
As he sat at the door with his pipe and his glass,
And thus to our friend did say;
'You destroy your health and senses too';
Says the grinder ' You're much too free,
Attend to your work, if you've ought to do,
And don't interfere with me.

There's many like you go sneaking about,
Persuading beer drinkers to turn!
'Tis easier far on our failing to spout,
Than by labour your living to earn;
I work when I like, and I play when I can,
And I envy no man I see,
Such chaps as you won't alter my plan,
For I know what agrees with me!'

Botanic Gardens   by E. Eaton, 1867.*

The subject of this truly excruciating piece of doggerel is John Law, who followed Robert Marnock curator of the Sheffield Botanical Gardens, and John Ewing who succeeded him. Opened in 1836, the gardens were only open to subscribers right until the Town Trust took them over in 1898 and so financial considerations loomed large in the early days. Ewing's greatest horticultural achievement was the successful cultivation of the great Victoria Regina lily in one of the pavilions. On one occasion he placed a chair on one of the leaves and sat on it!

> At Botanic Gardens, fixed with good intent,
> Is a braw Scot with inclination bent;
> He'd this in view, for he to Sheffield came,
> At Botanic Gardens saw a path to fame.
> There was a cloud he wished to dispel,
> 'Till that were done he saw that naught could go well.
> Tried every effort, every nerve he strung,
> To remove the debt that over the gardens hung.
> Plan after plan that showed his aim was good
> Applied to stars of lesser magnitude
> Then to his list he new subscribers get,
> So he removed the dark cloud of debt.
> A free trade glimmer soon began to play
> Up Glossop Road to 't Gardens took its way;
> The Sheffield chaps begun to fill the list;
> The Sheffield chaps begun to clear the mist.

* From 'Collected Poems' by E. Eaton, -The Fairyland Poet, Fuchsia Cottage, Palmerston Place, Grenoside.

The cloud removed, the aspect now is bright,
Great praise is due unto his northern light;
He in floral science with the foremost ranks,
So at your meetings vote him hearty thanks,
And take your Misses to them lovely cells,
Botanic Gardens where fair Flora dwells,
In beauty dressed, she all her friends delights,
By all her visitors she is much prized
And every nation that is civilised.
The curator's plan it appears has worked well,
A peep at Gardens thus will truly tell;
But peep again, and it may be truly said,
That Mr. Ewing's great improvements made.

Sheffield Park. Broadside Ballad
Printed by J.Pitts between 1819 and 1844

With these next two pieces I have clearly broken my own rule to include only verses that relate directly to the locality, for these two ballads are apparently connected to Sheffield only in the name. They could (and did) relate just as well to different parts of the country and have very familiar themes of love and betrayal. It is purely because they are such charming and typical examples of this form of popular entertainment that I feel compelled to include them here.

John Holland's House, Sheffield Park.

In Sheffield Park O there did dwell
A brisk young lad, I loved him well,
He courted me my heart to gain,
He is gone and left me full of pain.

I went upstairs to make the bed,
I laid me down and nothing said,
My mistress came and to me said,
What is the matter with you my maid?

O mistress, mistress you little know,
The pain and sorrow I undergo,
It's put your hand on my left breast,
My panting heart can take no rest.

My mistress away from me did go,
Some help, some help I will have for you,
No help, no help, no help I crave,
Sweet William brought me to my grave.

So take this letter to him with speed,
And give it to him if he can read,
And bring me an answer without delay
For he has stole my heart away.

She took the letter immediately,
He read it o'er while she stood by,
And soon he did the letter burn
Leaving this poor maid to make her mourn.

How could she think how fond I'd be
That I should fancy none but she,
Man was not made for one alone
I take delight to hear her mourn.

Then she returned immediately,
And found her maid as cold as clay
Beware young maids don't love in vain,
For love has broke her heart in twain.

She gathered the green grass for her bed
And a flowery pillow for her head
The leaves that blow from tree to tree
Shall be a covering for thee.

O cruel man, I find thou art,
For breaking my own child's heart,
Now she in Abraham's bosom sleeps,
While thy tormented soul shall weep.

First Brick House in Sheffield

The Sheffield Apprentice
Broadside Ballad, early Nineteenth Century

The following version of this traditional ballad was collected by Vaughan Williams in Norfolk in 1908 but versions of it appeared in broadside sheets throughout England in the early nineteenth century. There are versions in which the apprentice hails from Birmingham, London or even Cornwall so the local connection is tenuous at best, especially as it appears that it was a song which was especially popular amongst whaling crews!

I was brought up in Sheffield,
Though not of high degree;
My parents doted on me,
They had no child but me;
I roamed about for pleasure,
Where'er my fancy led,
Till I was bound apprentice,
Then all my joys were fled.

I did not like my master,
He did not use me well,
I made a resolution
Not long with him to dwell.
A wealthy rich young lady
From London met me there,
And offered me great wages
To serve her for a year.

I had not been in London
Scarce one month, two or three,
Before my honoured mistress
Grew very fond of me.
She said 'I've gold and silver,
I've houses and I've land
If you will marry me
They shall be at your command.'

'O no, dear honoured mistress
I cannot wed you now,
For I have lately promised
Likewise a solemn vow
To wed with dearest Polly
Your handsome chambermaid,
Excuse me honoured mistress,
She has my heart betrayed.'

She flew into a passion
And turned away from me,
Resolved within herself
She would be revenged on me;
Her gold ring from her finger,
As she was passing by,
She slipped into my pocket
And for it I must die.

For that before the justice,
The justice I was brought,
And there before the justice
I answered for my fault;
Long time I pleaded innocent
But that was all in vain,
She swore so false against me
That I was sent to gaol.

On the day of execution,
All on that fateful day,
I prayed the people round me
'O pray come pity me
Don't laugh at my downfall,
For I bid this world adieu;
Farewell my dearest Polly,
I died for love of you!'

Old houses, Town Head Street

Handsworth Sword Dancers*   by Joe Siddall, 1920.

By the badge ye shall know them, for they wear it with pride,
These dancers of Handsworth who are famed far and wide;
For that badge is the symbol that they have stood the test
For many long years, and still are the best
Troupe of sword dancers to be found in the land.
To see them in action, by gum, it is grand!
March, Clash, Snake and Single Sword Up,
And in Three Divide they are just warming up.
Then quickly they slip into Double Sword Down,
A difficult figure that has won them renoun.
And all through the figures they work like a clock,
And wind up the dance by making the Lock.
And the badges they wear are the locked swords, you see,
Presented to them by the E.F.D. Society
For the great display they gave at York,
Which for many day's after was all the town's talk,
J H Siddall is the Captain, and his brothers Joe, Walter and Will,
Along with Lomas, Barks and Staniforth are dancers of skill,
And little Verdon, whose front name is Pat,
A neat little dancer as quick as a cat;
And the musician, by name Tommy Gray,
Who while they are dancing, fine music does play.
And that's the full list of the dancers of note,
Who proudly carry the badge on their coat.

* The Handsworth Traditional Sword Dancers still perform their unique dance every Boxing Day outside Handsworth church.

Wednesdayites,

by Hazel Clarke, 1995

Wednesdayites are born that way
Seemingly they have no say
And all these little girls and boys
Soon outgrow their childhood toys.
Trotting off each Saturday
Keen to see their idols play,
Grown up, they are even more
Partisan than before.
Following their team around
Soon they've been to every ground
If Wednesday lose they're in despair,
A win, and they walk on air.
Lost games are blamed on the ref.
Of course, he was both blind and deaf.
But a win, and their hearts fill
With pride for their team's pure skill.
I'm sure that each Wednesdayite
Has no red blood, it's blue and white.

Sheffield Telegraph Series, 1904-5.

ALMOST "CROSSING THE BAR."

J. LYALL (Sheffield Wednesday).

Though ev'ry other man is passed,
It's Lyall curls them up at last;
His hands are prime, his nerve sublime,
He holds the fort and holds it fast.

HONOURS:
Helped to win the League Championship, 1902-3 and 1903-4.

Sheffield Telegraph Series, 1904-5.

THE WONDER-WORKER.

ERNEST NEEDHAM
(SHEFFIELD UNITED).

A better man than this you will not meet,
He plays the game with brains as well as feet;
The best of captains, quick, alert, and keen,
His equal in the way of half-backs, people say,
Has seldom on the football field been seen.

HONOURS:

Scotland, 1894, '5, '7, '8, '9, 1900, 1901. Wales, 1897, '8, '9, 1901, 1902.   Ireland, 1897, '9, 1900, 1901.
Helped to win the League Championship, 1897-8.
Helped to win the English Cup, 1899 and 1902.

The Whit Walk, by Grace Leeder-Jackson

The Whit Sing in Meersbrook Park, followed by the Sunday school treat, was so much a part of my family's annual calendar as a child that I find this poem particularly evocative.

In part of Yorkshire, once a year, we shared a special day,
But I believed the world could hear 'The Sing' on Whit Monday.
It started early with first light, we children rushed about,
Our sleepy eyes gazed with delight on our new clothes laid out.

Soon we were dressed and feeling smart, I know I looked quite prim,
'Till grandma did her rules impart "Keep fingers off that brim!"
I soon forgot her stern command as down to church we went,
We couldn't wait to hear the band, excitement was intent.

Then we were lined up in the lane, each standing four abreast,
No-one could blame us feeling vain, we all felt 'bestest dressed'.
Our altar boys, in surplice white, were standing well ahead,
Their task, to hold our banner right, denoting the church they led.

The colliery band marched down the hill, it gathered as it came,
From chapels up to Potter Hill right down to Mortomley Lane.
We were the last group joining on, our banner very small,
A pretty one, a dainty one, the chapel ones were tall.

With bubbling pride we marched along, hills seemed no longer steep,
The brass band played a marching song, we tried in step to keep,
The more crowds gathered on the way, our milkman and the baker,
Just everyone walked there that day to sing in the Ten Acre.

The Heroic and The Villainous

From the Rhyming Couplets of Worksop by Pigot, 15th Century.

These ancient verses read rather like clues to a medieval treasure hunt. They refer to the history of the de Furnivals, Lords of the Manor of Hallamshire during the thirteenth and fourteenth centuries. The name 'Molde' (or Maud in the modern spelling) appears twice. Maud de Lovetot, in marrying Gerard de Furnival, a crusading knight who died in Jerusalem in 1209, brought the manor into their possession and Maud Nevill, the daughter of Joan de Furnival and Thomas Nevill, brought the line to an end in marrying John Talbot, the hero of Shakespeare's Henry VII, in 1410. They had endowed Worksop Priory as the mother church to Sheffield, which is why the lords were buried there, and it is there that the mutilated monuments to which the poem refers can still be seen. The second verse here tells the extraordinary tale of how, when Gerard came home to his mother in 1237, with the news that Thomas her son had been killed in Palestine, she insisted that his brother return to bring home his remains for Christian burial!

> Good Molde was buryed most principal,
> Above Sir Thomas Nevill afore the hye autere;
> For a good doer most worthy of all
> That indued this place; and her husband infere:
> To reherse what she did, divers things sere,
> As expressed is afore, it would take long space:
> Bot in heaven therefore we trust there is place.

> When Sir Thomas was slayne for Christes sake,
> His broder came home, Gerarde agayne,
> And that Molde ther moder grevously gan take,
> That his bones emong hethen should be layne.
> And make him retorne without more disdeyne
> Againe to the holy land, and his bones home brought;
> As it was Goddes will that him dere boght.

Maud de Neville    *Thomas 'The Hasty' Furnival*

Then tumulate here in Nottinghamshire
At Wykesoppe, the north side of the mynster,
With his helm on his heade will enquire
With precious stones sometime that were set sers,
And a noble carbuncle on him doth he bere
On his hede; to see they may who so will,
Of my writing witness for to fulfil.

Thomas de Neville

Sir Gerard on the south side under a marbill stone
Near St.Peter's chapel is bered also;
And Sir William ther brother both flesh and bone
In our Lady chappell was bered even tho
In the midst of the chappell, good Molde a little fro;
Wyf to first Sir John (Gerrard) Fernival that was:
Which foresaid Sir William was gretely endured with grace.

Thomas, sterne and right hasty man,
The hasty Fournivall, but he was good founder
To the place of Wyrksoppe in his time than.
* * * * * * * * * * * *
Which foresaid Thomas on the north side is layde,
In a tomb of Alabaster, above the high Quere,
And William of the South side anens him is seid,
Here these two broder are buried in fere.

And Sir Thomas Nevill, treasorer of England,
Aboven the Quere is tumulate, his tomb is to see,
In the Middes for most royall there it doth stand,
And his doughter Molde of right high degree,
In Saynt Mary Chappell tumulate lyeth shee
Afore our blessed Lady, next the stall side,
There may she be seene, she is not to hyde.

Dame Johane is beryed aboven the hye quere,
Next Thomas Nevill that was her husband;
In alabaster an ymage sir Thomas right nere
As he is tumulate on his right hand.
And by her daughter Molde we understand
Went out the Fournivalls as by their name,
As Lovetots by Dame Molde afore did the same.

From Henry VI Part I
William Shakespeare.

The subject of this speech by a messenger to the assembled lords is John Talbot, who had become Lord of the Manor of Hallamshire with his marriage to Maud Nevill in 1410. Talbot was hailed as a great warrior in the French wars of Henry VI and served so heroically that he was created the First Earl of Shrewsbury by the King.

The tenth of August last this dreadful lord,
Retiring from the siege of Orleans,
Having full scarce six thousand in his troop,
By three and twenty thousand of the French
Was round encompassed and set upon.
No leisure had he to enrank his men;
He wanted pikes to set before his archers;
Instead, whereof, sharp stakes, plucked out of hedges,
They pitched in the ground confusedly,
To keep the horsemen off from breaking in.
More than three hours the fight continued;
Where valiant Talbot, above human thought,
Enacted wonders with his sword and lance:
Hundreds he sent to hell, and none durst stand him;
Here, there, and everywhere, enraged he flew:
The French exclaimed the devil was in arms;
All the whole army stood agazed on him:
His soldiers, spying his undaunted spirit,
A Talbot! A Talbot! Cried out amain,
And rushed into the bowels of the battle.

Later in the play the fortunes of war swing against the English. In Scene VI the following exchange takes place outside the gates of Bordeaux, which John Talbot, the king's great champion, who had been rewarded by the monarch in 1442 with the title of Earl of Shrewsbury, and his son, also John, had rashly been led to storm. Greatly outnumbered by the French they are both killed. Here Sir William Lucy comes with a herald following the battle to ascertain the score. The interchange is extremely reminiscent of those between the haughty St. George and his victims in the traditional English mummers plays.

In fact John Talbot and his son actually died at the Battle of Chatillon in 1453. His second son was killed at the Battle of Northampton in 1460.

Sir William Lucy

But where are the great Alcides of the field,
Valient Lord Talbot, Earl of Shrewsbury-
Created for his rare success in arms,
Great Earl of Washford, Waterford and Valence,
Lord Talbot of Goodrig and Urchinfield,
Lord Strange of Blackmere, Lord Verdun of Alton,
Lord Cromwell of Wingfield, Lord Furnival of Sheffield,
The thrice victorious Lord of Falconbridge;
Knight of the noble order of Saint George,
Worthy Saint Michael, and the Golden Fleece;
Great marshal to Henry the Sixth
Of all his wars within the realm of France?

La-Pucelle

Here is a silly-stately style indeed!
The Turk, that two and fifty kingdoms hath,
Writes not so tedious a style as this.-
Him that thou magnifiest with all these titles,
Stinking and fly-blown, lies here at our feet.

*John Talbot,
1st. Earl of Shrewsbury,
from the window in
the Cathedral.*

'An Epitaph upon the death of the noble Lord George Earle of Shrowsburye, who departed this mortall life the yere of our Lord God 1590, buried the eighteenth day of November.' Author unknown.*

One of Sheffield's greatest treasures is the remarkable ornate memorial to George, the 6th Earl of Shrewsbury, the custodian of Mary Queen of Scots, in the Cathedral. Beside it, at one time, hung a board with the following verse painted on it. The board itself vanished long ago but fortunately the antiquarian Roger Dodsworth recorded the verse in the 17th century.

> George Earle of Shrowsbury, Washford and Waterford,
> Erle Marshall of England, Talbot of Goodridge, Lord
> > Verdon of Altoun, Furnival of Sheffield,
> > Lord Luftot of Worksopp, Lord Crumbwell of
> > Wingfield.
>
> Lord Strange of the Blackmeere, and Justice by North Trent
> Of forests and chases, a councillor, President
> > Unto his soveraine Quene, &c., for his loyalty
> > Knight of the garter, eke these titles all had hee;
>
> Which solemnly proclaimed by heralds that daie
> When was his funeral; with honour every day.
> > Lefetenant of Stafford and Darbyshire also
> > In days most dangerouse he was assigned tho.
>
> A mighty man he was, in wealth he did abound
> Of all his howse therein the like was never found:
> > He fast was to his friend, and heavy to his foe;
> > He lived so direct that none could worke him woe.
>
> The poore mans plaint to here his eares would alwaise bend,
> And them in there cause against there foes defend.
> > Five hundred pound he gave for ever to remaine
> > To Chesterfield to help poor trasdesmen without gaine.
>
> But ever he lay full his country to defend,
> And never did oppresse whereby he might offend.
> > Marie Queen of Scots then vanquished att home
> > In battill, unto us for succour first did come:

* Quoted in Hunter's 'Hallamshire' 1819.

When she by seaventeen yeares abode with this great peer,
Until against her realme to worke she did conspire
    Great things; whereof by Lords thrice tenn and six of name,
    She tainted was at last and suffered for the same.

Soe great a trust as this so long was never seene,
A subject for to be a keeper of a Queene.
    To scape out his hand by divers waiss she sought;
    But still he did prevent the waies that she had wrought:

For wisely he did see what peril might have been
If she had scapt away, to realm or eke to Queene:
    Wherefore he showed himselfe most carefull for to be,
    Soe great a charge to keep with all fidelity.

Whereby he hath preserved his name of soe great renowne;
The Talbot ever true and faithful to the crowne.
    But yet for all his wealth his honour and his fame,
    Loe where he lies in earth from whence at first he came.

The Monument to George, 6th Earl of Shrewsbury, in Sheffield Cathedral.

Song of the Anglo-Saxons on the Victory of Brunanburgh
from Anglo-Saxon Chronicle, translated by Ingram, London, 1823

The following poem, which, incidentally, I think needs to be recited out loud for best effect, refers to the invasion of the Anglo-Saxon kingdom to the south of the line from the Mersey to the Don by the combined forces of the king of Scotland, Constantine, and the Viking, Olaf of York, then residing in Dublin, in the year 937AD. There is a long-standing tradition that this, the bloodiest battle of the era, was waged on soil to the east of Sheffield, between Catcliffe and Brinsworth, although the evidence for this is purely circumstantial. The result was a stunning victory for King Athelstan against overwhelming odds whereby the unification of the Anglo-Saxon kingdom was achieved.

Athelstan, King
of Earls the lord
rewarder of heroes,
and his brother eke,
Edmund Atheling,
elder of ancient race
slew
with the edge of their swords,
the foe at Brumby.
the sons of Edward
their board-walls clove,
and hewed their banners.
So were they taught
by kindred zeal,
that they at camp oft,
'gainst any robber,
their land should defend,
their hordes and homes.
Pursuing fell
the Scottish clans;
the men of the fleet
in numbers fell;
'midst the din of the field,
the warrior swate.
Since the sun was up
in morning tide,
gigantic light!
Glad over grounds,

God's candle bright,
eternal Lord!
'tell the noble creature
sat in the western main
there lay many
of the Northern heroes
under a shower of arrows,
shot over shields;
and Scotland's boast,
a Scythian race,
the mighty seed of Mars!
With chosen troops,
throughout the day
the West Saxons fierce
pressed on the loathed bands;
hew'd down the fugitives,
and scattered the rear,
with mill-sharpened blades.
The Mercians too
the hard hand-play
spared not to any
of those that with Anlaf
over the briny deep
in the ship's bosom
sought this land
for the hardy fight.
Five kings lay
in the field of battle
in the bloom of youth
pierced with swords.
So seven eke
of the earls of Anlaf;
and of the ship's crew
unnumber'd crowds.
There was dispersed
the little band
of hardy Scots
the dread of Northern hordes,
urged by the noisy deep,
by unrelenting fate!
The king of the fleet
with his slender craft
escaped with his life
on the felon flood.
and so too Constantine
the valiant chief
returned to the north
in hasty flight.

The Dragon of Wantley
Traditional, 17th Century

If John Talbot comes down through history as the greatest heroic figure to be linked to Sheffield's past, More of More Hall, the dragon slayer in this next poem, surely deserves to be better known as the locality's greatest fictional hero. This story, originating from the Don valley to the north of Sheffield around Wharncliffe Crags, is not as well known as it was in the past. Indeed in 1737 it was turned into a comic opera by Henry Carey and performed in Covent Garden, to the delight of Handel. It is not the straight forward traditional folk tale it appears. The exact origins of the piece are, understandably, obscure but it appears to have been composed following the long legal wrangles and land disputes between the lords of the manor, the Wortleys (here characterised as the dragon) and their tenants, culminating in some extremely unpleasant incidents in the 1590s.

The poem has been reproduced many times. This version comes from Bishop Thomas Percy's *'Reliques of Ancient English Poetry'*, 1827.

    Old stories tell how Hercules
        A dragon slew at Lerna,
    With seven heads, and fourteen eyes,
        To see and well discern-a;
    But he had a club, this dragon to drub,
        Or he had ne'er done it, I warrant ye;
    But More of More Hall, with nothing at all,
        He slew the dragon of Wantley.

    This dragon he had two furious wings,
        Each one upon each shoulder;
    With a sting in his tayl as long as a flayl,
        Which made him bolder and bolder.
    He had long claws, and in his jaws
        Four and forty teeth of iron;
    With a hide as tough as any buff,
        Which did him round environ.

    Have you not heard how the Trojan horse
        Held seventy men in his belly?
    This dragon was not quite as big,
        But very near, I'll tell ye.
    Devoured he poor children three,
        That could not with him grapple,
    And at one sup he ate them up,
        As one would eat an apple.

All sorts of cattle this dragon did eat;
    Some say he ate up trees,
And that the forests sure he would,
    Devour up by degrees.
For houses and churches to him were geese and turkeys,
    He ate all and left none behind,
But some stones, dear Jack, that he could not crack,
    Which on the hill you will find.

In Yorkshire, near fair Rotherham,
    The place, I know it well,
Some two or three miles, or thereabouts,
    I vow I cannot tell;
But there is a hedge, just on the hill edge,
    And Matthew's house hard by it,
O there and then was the dragon's den,
    You would not choose but spy it.

The Dragon's Den, Wharncliffe Crags, from Pawson & Brailsford's Guide, 1862

Some say this dragon was a witch;
    Some say he was a devil,
For from his nose a smoke arose,
    And with it burning snivel;
Which he cast off, when he did cough,
    In a well that he did stand by;
Which made it look, just like a brook
    Running with burning brandy.

Hard by a furious knight there dwelt,
    Of whom all towns did ring;
For he could wrestle, play at quarter-staff, kick, cuff and huff,
    Call a son of a whore, do any kind of a thing:
By the tail and the mane, with his hands twain,
    He swung a horse till he was dead;
And that which is stranger, for his very anger,
    Eat him all up but his head.

These children, as I am told, being eat;
    Men, women, girls and boys,
Sighing and sobbing, came to his lodging,
    And made a hideous noise:
'O save us all, More of More Hall,
    Thou peerless knight of these woods;
Do thou but slay this dragon, who won't leave us a rag on,
    We'll give thee all our goods.'

'Tut, tut,' quoth he, 'no goods I want;
    But I want, I want, in sooth,
A fair maid of sixteen, that's brisk and keen,
    With smiles about the mouth;
Hair black as sloe, skin white as snow,
    With blushes her cheek adorning;
To anoint me o'er night, ere I go to fight,
    And to dress me in the morning.'

This being done, he did engage
    To hew the dragon down;
But first he went new armour to
    Bespeak at Sheffield town;
The spikes all about, not within but without,
    Of steel so sharp and strong,
Both behind and before, arms, legs and all o'er,
    Some five or six inches long.

Had you but seen him in this dress,
    How fierce he looked and how big,
You would have thought him for to be
    Some Egyptian porcupig:
He frightened all, cats, dogs and all,
    Each cow, each horse and each hog:
For fear they did flee, for they took him to be
    Some strange outlandish hedge-hog.

To see this fight, all people then
    Got up on trees and houses,
On churches some, and chimneys too,
    But these put on their trowses,
Not to spoil their hose. As soon as he rose,
    To make him strong and mighty,
He drank by the tale, six pots of ale,
    And a quart of aqua-vitae.

It is not strength that always wins
    For wit doth strength excel ;
Which made our cunning champion
    Creep down into a well ;
Where he did think, this dragon would drink,
    And so he did in truth ;
And as he stooped low, he rose up and cried 'Boh!'
    And hit him in the mouth.

'O,' quoth the dragon, 'pox take thee, come out,
    Thou disturb'st me in my drink.'
And then he turned and s... at him;
    Good lack, how he did stink!
Beshrew thy soul, thy body's foul,
    Thy dung smells not like balsam;
Thou son of a whore, thou stink'st so sore,
    Sure thy diet is unwholesome.

Our politick knight, on the other side,
    Crept out upon the brink,
And gave the dragon such a douse,
    He knew not what to think:
'By cock,' quoth he, 'say you so : do you see ?'
    And then at him he let fly
With hand and foot, and so they went to't;
    And the word it was Hey boys, hey!

'Your words,' quoth the dragon, 'I don't understand ;'
    Then to it they fell at all,
Like two wild boars so fierce, if you may,
    Compare great things with small.
Two days and a night, with this dragon did fight
    Our champion on the ground;
Tho' their strength it was great, their skill it was neat,
    They never had one wound.

At length the hard earth began to quake,
    The dragon gave him a knock,
Which made him to reel, and straightway he thought
    To lift him as high as a rock,
And thence let him fall. But More of More Hall,
    Like a valiant son of Mars,
As he came like a lout, so he turned him about,
    And hit him a kick on the a.....

'O' quoth the dragon, with a deep sigh,
    and turned six times together,
sobbing and tearing, cursing and swearing
    out of his throut of leather;
'More of More Hall! O thou rascal!
    Would I had seen thee never;
With the thing at thy foot, thou hast pricked my a….gut,
    And I'm quite undone forever.'

'Murder, murder' the dragon cried,
    'Alack, alack, for grief;
Had you but missed that place, you could
    Have done me no mischief'
Then his head he shaked, trembled and quaked,
    And down he laid and cried;
First on one knee, the on back tumbled he,
    So groaned, kicked, s…., and died.

Wharncliffe from Table Rock by William Ibbett

As a footnote to this ballad it is worth recording that **Samuel Roberts**, the Sheffield Member of Parliament, in 1838 was moved to compose and publish an updated version of the Dragon of Wantley, which he called **'The New Dragon of Wharncliffe'**. The impetus for this was the fury that he felt on the defeat of the Bill to prohibit the setting of loaded spring guns by landowners to deter trespassers and poachers. The Bill was defeated at its third reading in the Lords in 1824 by a single vote, that of the Earl of Wharncliffe! A few verses from Samuel Robert's very clever parody will suffice to give a flavour of the depth of his anger.

    The Dragon in his den secure
    With Mrs. D did dwell,
    And many little Dragonetts,
    All looking mighty well.

    For they did eat the best of meat
    That Wharncliffe Chase could boast of
    They'd fallow deer throughout the year,
    With game a numerous host of.

    Oh happy had it been, and well
    For all the country round,
    Had Wharncliffe's dragon been content
    With game which he there found.

    But he did sigh for other fry
    All to afford him pleasure,
    And took delight, both day and night,
    To make them bounce their last time.

Old men, with grief and age stone blind,
With little lads to lead them,
Old women, hobbling without lads,
Though seeming much to need them.

Young lovers too, inclined to woo,
All in the lovely moonlight,
With children gay, in morning play,
Right glad it was so soon light.

All these, with very many more,
That in these woods did stray,
The dragon all for love of sport,
Without remorse did slay.

Mid bushes he where none could see
By day and night abides,
With balls of lead to shoot them dead
Or surely bang their hides.

It Mrs. Dragon much did grieve
That he should flee from billing,
That she alone, should lie and moan,
While he was children killing.

Bill Brown, The Poacher
Broadsheet Ballad, early nineteenth century.

A number of the poems in this collection refer to the hostility between nineteenth century landowners and poachers. On a number of occasions this led to bloodshed, violence and even murder, as this ballad relates.

In seventeen hundred and sixty nine,
    As plainly doth appear then,
A bloody scene was felt most keen,
    Till death it did draw near then;
Of poor Bill Brown, of Brightside Town,
    A lad of well-known fame then,
Who took delight, both day and night,
    To trace the timid hare then.

With wires strong they marched along,
    Unto brave Thriberg town then,
With nut brown ale they ne'er did fail,
    And many a health went round then,
Brave Luna bright did shine that night,
    To the woods they did repair then,
True as the sun their dogs did run,
    To trace the lofty hare then.

A lofty breeze amongst the trees,
    While shining he came on then,
Like Cain he stood seeking for blood
    With his bayonet and his gun then.
Then he did charge, with shot quite large,
    George Miller did him spy then,
This rogue's intent was fully bent,
    One of us poor lads should die then.

His cruel hand he did command,
    That instant for to fire then,
And so with strife took poor Brown's life,
    Which once he thought entire then.
His blood aloud for vengeance cried,
    The keeper came he on then,
Like cruel Cain up to him came,
    And so renewed his wounds then.

Now this dear soul ne'er did controul,
    Nor think that man no ill then,
But to Dalton Brook his mind was stuck,
    While his clear blood did spill then;

No one there nigh him stood then,
And there he lay till break of day,
    Dogs licking his dear blood then.

Farewell, dear heart, now I must part,
    From wife and children dear ten,
Pity my doom, it was too soon,
    That ever I came here then;
Farewell unto the brave dear lads,
    Whoever range the fields then,
This cruel man's murdering hand,
    Has caused me to yield then.

In grief and pain till death it came,
    To embrace his dear soul then,
Which took its flight to heaven straight,
    Where no man can contoul then
The country round heard of the sound,
    Of poor Brown's blood being spilled then,
'Twas put in vogue, to find the rogue
    That justice might be done then.

With irons strong he was marched along,
    Unto York Castle fair then,
In a dark cell was doomed to dwell,
    Till the judge he did appear then;
George Miller bold, as I've been told,
    Deny it here who can then,
He ne'er was loth to take his oath,
    Brown was a murdered man then.

There was a man who there did stand,
    Whose heart did shake amain then,
But gold did fly they can't deny
    Or at Tyburn he'd been hung then;
They'd ne'er been bold to hear it told,
    To hear of Shirtley's doom then,
The judge put off to God on high,
    Or he might have judged him soon then.

There brave Ned Greaves ne'er did fail,
    To crown poor Bill Brown's name then,
George Miller brave defies each knave
    That travels o'er the plain then;
With sword and gun now he will run,
    Though the law it doth maintain then,
Yet poor Brown's blood lost in the wood,
    For vengeance cries amain, then.

Sheffield Children's Skipping Rhyme, recalling the hanging of Charlie Peace, the Banner Cross Murderer in 1879.

I love Charlie

Charlie was a thief

Charlie killed a copper,

Charlie came to grief.

When the coppers caught him

They hanged him on a rope,

Poor old Charlie,

You haven't got a hope.

Frank Fearne   by Joseph Mather, 1782

Fearne was executed at York assizes on March 27th 1782 and afterwards gibbeted on Loxley Edge for the murder of Nathan Andrews, a respectable watchmaker who had a shop in the High Street. A surprising number of the old gravestones in the churchyard of Loxley Chapel still bear the family name.

> Mortals all in town or city,
> Pay attention to this truth;
> Let your bowels yearn with pity,
> Towards a poor deluded youth.
>
> Tho' with Satan's vile injunctions,
> I was forced to comply,
> Now it causes sad reflections,
> Since I am condemned to die.
>
> Andrews, O that name! It pierces,
> Thro' my very inmost soul;
> And my torments much increases,
> In this gloomy condemned hole.
>
> At Kirk Edge I shot and stabbed him,
> Cut his throat and bruised his pate,
> Of his watch and money robbed him,
> Causes my unhappy fate.
>
> Christians pray that true repentance
> May be given a wretch like me.
> I acknowledge my just sentence,
> There's no law can set me free.
>
> Let me make one observation,
> Though to sin I've been enslaved,
> Through my saviour's mediation,
> My poor soul may yet be saved.
>
> Hark! I'm called to execution,
> And must bid the world adieu!
> 'Tis the hour of dissolution,
> And my moments are but few.
>
> Let me endless bliss inherit,
> Wash me from my guilty stains;
> O, receive my precious spirit,
> Though my body hang in chains.

Stevens and Lastley's Execution. by Joseph Mather, 1790

Mather's response to the hanging of John Stevens and Thomas Lastley, for what amounted to little more than a misfired practical joke, strikes a very different tone to that of the 'just' execution of Frank Fearne. He does not mince his words in condemning such a brutal sentence. The prank for which they were to lose their lives occurred on the evening of Saturday August 29th, 1789 on which four button makers, Lastley, Stevens, Michael Bingham, John Booth and a labourer, John Wharton had spent the evening drinking in The White Hart in Waingate. Wharton left the group and purchased some provisions in the market. The others caught up with him with the intention of persuading him to return to the pub. When Wharton went into the urinal on Lady's Bridge, leaving his basket of goods outside, the others ran off with it to The Barrel Inn, where Stevens lodged, and asked the landlady to cook a piece of lamb which was in it. It is said that they expected Wharton to join them and left money to pay for it when he did not do so. In the meanwhile Wharton had actually gone to the constable. The culprits were caught, brought before the magistrate and the grim events proceeded.

Few expected the prosecution to proceed towards a death penalty and when it did for Stevens, Lastley and Booth in March 1790, the town was outraged. Feelings ran high against Wharton who was forced to flee Sheffield after an angry mob, no doubt including Mather, wrecked his home, accusing him of betraying his workmates for the sake of the £40 reward payable on securing a conviction for robbery. A public meeting was called and a petition to the king organised by the Master Cutler. Tragically, the reprieve which was granted arrived two days after the execution, the messenger having been held up by flooding on the road. Bingham had previously been reprieved by the judge.

O Wharton, thou villain, most base,
   Thy name must eternally rot;
Poor Stevens and Lastley's sad case
   Forever thy conscience will blot.
These victims, thou wickedly sold,
   And into eternity hurl'd,
For lucre of soul sinking gold,
   To set thee on foot in the world.

Thy house is a desolate place,
   Reduc'd to a shell by the crowd,
Destruction pursues thee apace,
   While innocent blood cries aloud.
Poor Booth in strong fetters thou'st left
   Appointed for Botany Bay,
He is of all comforts bereft,
   To die by a hair's breadth each day.

Depend on't thou never can'st thrive,
   Thy sin will e're long find thee out,
If not whilst thy body's alive'
   It will after death, without doubt.
When Stevens and Lastley appears,
   Requiring their blood at thy hands,
Tormenting a million of years,
   Can't satisfy justice's demands.

Some others were equally vile,
   To prompt thee to this wicked work;
In order to share in the spoil,
   Thou got by the blood spilt at York.
All are equally guilty with thee,
   And as a reward for their pains,
They ought to be hung on a tree,
   And then be suspended in chains

A further footnote to this sad event is provided by the fact that George Moore was hanged along with Stevens and Lastley. He was a blade forger, well known by the Sheffield crowd for his prize-fighting skills. He was convicted of breaking into a hardware shop in York. The following extract is from a poem written by James Montgomery as he resided in York gaol in 1796. How many times have we heard this excuse?

>I, George Moore, must tell you plain,
>>I lose my life for little gain;
>For shopbreaking that shameful deed,
>>It makes my tender heart to bleed;
>A harlot's company I did keep,
>>To think of her that makes me weep;
>Through her I took to evil ways,
>>Which is the short'ning of my days.

Sir Francis Chantrey   by Ellen Styring, 1930s.

Francis Chantrey, born in 1781 in a little cottage at Jordanthorpe, rose to become the most acclaimed sculptor of the early nineteenth century. The story has often been told of how he worked as a boy delivering the milk to the town and as an assistant to a grocer in Fargate before becoming apprenticed to the carver and gilder, Robert Ramsey, in High Street. In 1802 he set up on his own account as a portrait painter in a house in the corner of Paradise Square. He later moved to London and a list of those whose memorials he sculpted would include virtually every notable of the time, including four reigning monarchs, George III, George IV, William IV and Queen Victoria. The area around Norton Church, outside which stands a large obelisk to his memory, is frequently referred to as 'Chantreyland

> We proudly honour Chantrey's name
> Great sculptor he of Sheffield fame,
> > Commanded by a king
> > His finest work to bring.
> In Lichfield Church so exquisite and free,
> His 'Sleeping Children' there enshrined you see.
>
> As boy he carried milk to town,
> And daily rode his donkey down,
> > Small figures made of clay,
> > Beuguiled him by the way,
> 'Tis said, on Shalesmoor he has often strayed
> To see some special models there displayed.
>
> As youth he roamed to Sheaf-Ground Hall
> On some fair lady there to call,
> > But his artistic eye
> > Could not his art deny,
> And truly great the model he prepared
> The statue ordered by King George the Third.

His monument to William Pitt
For London's Square is nobly fit.
    His Lady Russell fair,
    Few can with this compare;
And far in Boston State House you will find
His statue of George Washington enshrined.

The shades of Chantrey's power you mark
In Steven's famed in Weston Park,
    And Green whose art so fair,
    Framed mantel pieces rare,
And other great designers you will find
Who drew their influence from the master mind.

A man whose skill throughout his days,
From nations won the highest praise.
    We visit Chantrey Land
    His fame on every hand.
His noble statues in Cathedrals fair
His lowly tomb in little Norton there.

Great Chantrey, knight of true renown
With patience won the sculptor's crown,
    Designs throughout the land,
    Your pure delight command,
The great Westminster Abbey owns his fame,
But Sheffield always must Sir Francis claim.

Chantrey's Memorial to the Harrisons in Sheffield Cathedral

*From 'Rhymes of Old Sheffield' Published by Leng & Co. Sheffield.

The Ballad of Spence Broughton the Highwayman.
19th Century

This song was reproduced in Mr. Frank Kidson's Traditional Tunes in 1891, though the unhappy subject goes back 100 years earlier. It tells the dying words of Spence Broughton, the infamous highwayman who was executed in 1792 in York for his part in robbing the Sheffield to Rotherham mail. The truly grisly part of the story is not told in this song, for his body was brought back to Sheffield and hung on a gibbet for the next 36 years at the site of the crime. The spot has been immortalised by having been named Broughton Lane. Some have been heard to say that the parking charges for the Arena car park which now occupies the position are a greater case of highway robbery than that for which Spence was hung!

Attercliffe Road. Broughton's gibbet appears on the right.

To you, my dear companions, accept these lines, I pray:
A most impartial trial has occurred this day;
'Tis from your dying Broughton, to show this wretched fate
Pray, make your reformation before it is too late.

The loss of your companion will grieve your hearts full sore,
I know that my fair Ellen will my wretched fate deplore;
Thinking of those happy hours that now are past and gone,
That I, unhappy Broughton, would I had ne'er been born.

Brought up in wicked habits, which wrought in me no fear,
How little did I think that my time had been so near;
But now I am overtaken, I am bound and cast to die,
Exposed, a bad example to all that does pass by.

O, that I had but gone unto some far distant clime,
Then a gibbet post for Broughton would never have been mine;
But as for such like wishes, they are vanity and vain,
Alas! It is but folly and madness to complain.

One night to try and slumber I closed my weeping eyes,
I heard a foot approaching, which struck me with surprise;
I listened for a moment, a voice made this reply,
'Prepare thyself, Spence Broughton, tomorrow thou must die'.

Farewell my wife and children, to you I say adieu,
I never should have come to this had I stayed at home with you;
But I hope, through my redeemer, to gain a happy shore,
Farewell, farewell for ever, Spence Broughton is no more.

References to Collected Works and Sources.

Francis Buchanan, Sheffield Castle and Sheffield Manor, from *'Sparks from Sheffield Smoke: a series of local and other poems'*, **1882.**

Edward Carpenter, Sheffield, in *'Towards Democracy, Part 4: Who shall command the Heart?'* **1902.**
Carpenter's poetry reflects his deeply held beliefs as a Christian socialist. He moved to the Sheffield area and settled in Millthorpe in the Cordwell Valley in 1883. He died in 1929.

Darbyshire, E. Sheffield Farewell, Opening of Firth Park, My Old House by the Don and Impromptu from *'Ballads, Poems and Recitations', pub. Wrigley, Sheffield,* **1885.**
Derbyshire was an optician who had a shop on Bow Street. Amongst his collection are the verses with the unlikely titles of 'Granny to her Specs' and 'Turkey Stuffing'!

Senior, Joseph, (The Smithy Bard) Invitation, Cutler's Daughter and The Whittlesmith's Lamentation from *'Smithy Rhymes and Stithy Chimes', pub. Leader, Sheffield,* **1882.**
Senior was a blade forger at Joseph Rodgers Norfolk Street works. He was encouraged to publish his poems to help support himself as his eyesight was failing.

Brufton, H.P. (T'Owd Hammer) Hungry Forties, from *'Sheffield Dialect and Other Poems',* **1937.**
The poems were originally written for radio broadcast.

Ebenezer Downing (T'Stooaker) Street March of the Sheffield Boy's Brigade from *'Smoak thru' a Shevvield Chimla',* **1906.**

Ellen Styring. Sir Francis Chantrey and Sir Henry Coward from *'Rhymes of Old Sheffield'* pub. Leng, Sheffield, **1935.**

John Hall ('J.H.J.') The Steam Hammer, and The Toll Keeper from *'Thoughts and Sketches in Verse', pub. Pawson and Brailsford, Sheffield,* **1891.**

William Dowsing. The Old Canal, The Tip and A Street Scene from *'Sheffield Vignettes, A Series of Sonnets', pub. Northend, Sheffield,* **1910.**

Henry Waterfall, My Native Rivelin from *'Rivelin Rhymes', pub. Robertshaw, Sheffield,* **1880.**

Index Of First Lines

A few months since on frolic bent, ...137
A large crowd gathered on the hillside ...127
A stately pile is raised, new civic home ...56
Alone, here oft may Scotia's beauteous Queen ...21
A man called How of Southend town, ...87
Amidst an avenue of haunting shades ...75
An early moon was near its height, ...122
April laughs in England, ...138
At Botanic Gardens, fixed with good intent, ...144
Athelstan, king, of Earls the Lord, ...163
At the Bowling Green the meeting was held, ...107
At Trumpington, near Cambridge, ...86
Aw'm sickened o' hearin'o't' 'gooid owd toimes' ...77

Be silent my anvil and hammer, ...106
Beneath this stone a grinder lies. ...129
But where are the great Alcides of the field, ...160
By the badge ye shall know them, for they wear it with pride ...150

Come blind Andrew Turner! Link in mine thy time-tired arm, ...47
Come, let us raise a monument, ...50
Corruption tells me homicide ...48
Cum all yo cuttlin heroes, where'ersome'er yo be ...140
Cushla! Cushla! Cushla! 'tis the soul of you I'm wanting, ...62

Dad, the kettle's boiling, ...69

Five rivers, like the fingers of a hand, ...18
For years and years you've served us well, ...70

George Earle of Shrowsbury, Washford and Waterford, ...161
Good Molde was buryed most principal, ...156

Hail Sheffield! Happy, good, old-fashion'd town, ...9
Here lies a man that was Knott born ...131
Here they come with a tap of drum,- ...60
Here's to the lads of the A. R. P. ...126
High dormers are rising ...35
High on the Longshawe Moors, ...109

I cannot hail thee, tho' thou liv'st in story,- 43
I dream of my childhood, of days long since gone, ... 25
I love Charlie 174
I was brought up in Sheffield, ... 148
I, Lord Furnival, ... 42
I'm a blade, rough handled, fluted and spangled, ... 93
In all their pride still wave the Wharncliffe's woods 10
In a fair country stands a filthy town, ... 76
In ancient Sheffield by the Don, ... 33
In death divided from their dearest kin, ... 112
In part of Yorkshire, once a year, we shared a special day, ... 153
In seventeen hundred and sixty nine, ... 172
In Sheffield market, I declare, ... 81
In Sheffield Park O there did dwell 146
In the rain, the rhythms of the water, ... 92
It is thy stream so fair I see 23
It's the wonder of wonders, this mighty steam hammer, ... 99

John Brown & Co are famous men, ... 103

Let me sing of the joys of Cole's Corner 64
Like Nimrod I did range the field 131

'Mid heavy smoke wreaths black as witchery 55
Mortals all in town or city, ... 175
My Scythe and hammer lies reclin'd 131

No name hast thou, lone streamlet, ... 22

O Wharton, thou villain, most base, ... 177
Of good Sir Henry here we sing, ... 59
Oh let our hill re-echo, ... 51
Oh! What a lovely summer, ... 68
Old Sheffield, my birthplace, I'm leaving behind me, ... 40
Old stories tell how Hercules 164
Ordained I was a beggar, ... 79
Our cutlery's created from Sheffield's finest steel, ... 88

Ring ye bells, till ye rock your steeples! 57

Sarah and William Adams! Here we stood 15

Sheffield is a city without a zoo	32
Sheffield, once proud city	39
Sheffield, smoke involved; dim where she stands	12
Sheffield was the place	8
Since first from iron	84
Stop, for the ground is holy here;	45
The bloody fields of Waterloo	132
The brave horses yield,	130
The muscle, the brain, the blood of our sons,	26
The Rose and Crown In Sheffield town,	136
The Sheffield grinder's a terrible blade,	96
The stars hung high o'er Loxley Vale, the cattle sought the shed,	119
The tenth of August last this dreadful lord,	159
The voice of nature here prevailed	17
There was remembrance dimly paints its form	19
There was a fox sat in his den,	81
There was a jolly Grinder once,	142
There's to be two ventilators	80
This young man's health, an it shall gooa rahnd,	90
Throughout the world Sheffield was steel,	37
Thud! Thud! Thud!	101
To be a Sheffield grinder it is no easy life,	97
To England's future king	53
To you, my dear companions, accept these lines, I pray:	181
T'was the dead of the night,	115
Unwashed, unkempt, half clothed, half shod, they stand,	78
Up! sluggards up! the mountains one by one	14
Wednesdayites are born that way	151
What makes this Government lay waste	67
We proudly honour Chantrey's name	179
When summer comes on and the sweet month of June,	16
Where a spur of the moors runs forward into the great town,	72
Where sooty tops of clanking tilts arise,	13
Where toils the mill by ancient woods embraced,	95
We went to the City Hall to see the Beatles,	66
We who tamed the fires that flamed	89
Ye Vet'rans of Sheffield, with intellects bright,	28

***

Printed in Great Britain
by Amazon